Realistic Model Railroad
OPERATION

How to run your trains like the real thing

Tony Koester

KALMBACH
BOOKS

Printed in the United States of America

03 04 05 06 07 08 09 10 11 12   10 9 8 7 6 5 4 3 2 1

Visit our website at
http://kalmbachbooks.com
Secure online ordering available.

Publisher's Cataloging-in-Publication
(Provided by Quality Books, Inc.)

Koester, Tony.
     Realistic model railroad operation / Tony Koester.
     p. cm.
     ISBN 0-89024-418-9

     1. Railroads—Models. 2. Railroads—Management.
  I. Title.

TF197.K64 2003   625.1'9
                    QBI02-200887

Art director: Kristi Ludwig
Book design: Sabine Beaupré

All photos unless otherwise noted are by Tony Koester

Contents

Introduction

"Realistic operation" is nothing more than the use of models in a manner that complements the realism and care that went into their construction. Every move has a purpose. Here the author uncouples the Low Gap Shifter's Mallet from its train so it can work a lineside tipple on the Coal Fork Extension of the Allegheny Midland.

"Realistic operation" is a term model railroaders use to mean the movement of scale models of cars and trains in a systematic, realistic manner by performing several of the more interesting jobs done by professional railroaders. The purpose of this book is to help you understand why so many of us enjoy realistic operation on our railroads as well as how you can operate your own layout more realistically.

To an increasing number of modelers, realistic operation is the ultimate goal of the hobby. It allows us to use our models in ways that complement their realism. Action has always been the focal point of model railroading, regardless of scale or gauge, and realistic operation simply guides that action so as to emulate the movement of people and cargo on full-size railroads.

Whether you have or are building a scale model railroad or prefer to run hi-rail equipment, realistic operation can enhance your enjoyment of and appreciation for our broad-shouldered hobby.

Realistic operation is really about making a series of simple, logical, common-sense decisions. In fact, after you read through the several pages of our Quick-Start Guide (Chapter 2), you'll find that you can actually operate your railroad today. Once you've mastered a few basics, it may be time to move on to more sophisticated approaches to operation, but feel free to stop at

any point along the road. There's no final exam, no one best way to operate your railroad, any more than there is a best railroad to model.

In fact, I have long believed that trying to identify and make a "best" choice is counterproductive. Too often, we waste countless hours in worrisome deliberations that could be applied to being enjoyably productive. It's better, in my view, to do a reasonable amount of homework, identify a few options, make a good choice, and then work hard to convert that good choice into a *great* choice—something you can enjoy for a long time.

So it is with realistic operation. There are quite a few approaches to operating model railroads, and the pages of this book could easily be filled with detailed descriptions of each of them. Instead, I have chosen to review the basic principles behind and goals of realistic operation, then describe a perennially popular method of car forwarding: car cards and waybills. Rest assured

that you can apply the general principles behind this system to almost any method of moving cars realistically, as it is firmly grounded in prototype practices. Other chapters review the basics of operation, short cuts, dispatching, and signaling, plus an overview of an operating session. Terminology definitions and other helpful reference material is provided in the Appendix.

This book contains more than enough information on realistic operation to get you started, but it won't tell you everything you'll ever need and want to know. I haven't learned it all myself yet, and what applies to Railroad A may be at odds with the rules and conventions of Railroad B. That's the best part, however: There's always something new to learn about operation. This will help to keep your interest level high for years to come.

Whatever your interests, whatever the scale and gauge of your models, whatever type and era of railroading interests you most, operation

"Operation" implies purposefully moving trains and individual cars as well as emulating the more challenging railroad jobs. Here a Western Maryland local crew sets out a boxcar in Parsons, W. Va., in the 1970s.

is a major enhancement of the modeling process. Moreover, realistic operation is like getting something for nothing: You've bought and built and detailed and weathered models that interest you. Now it's time to use them in a manner that more fully reflects their innate realism!

One more thing before we get started: Take time to read through the Appendix, as it contains a lot of useful information. In fact, treat it as a homework assignment, as this book is only a primer on the myriad ways to enjoy our hobby through realistic operation.

—*Tony Koester*

CHAPTER ONE

Realistic models, realistic movements

Fig. 1-1: Action is at the heart of operation, but only when it adds a sense of purpose to the movement of cars and trains.

You're at the threshold of one of the most exciting adventures in model railroading, or any model-building hobby, for that matter: using your models in a manner that fully reflects their realism and capabilities. Model railroad equipment is, after all, designed and built not to gather dust on a mantelpiece but to run (fig. 1-1). Running trains realistically is called "operation," and it adds a lot of utility to your models at virtually no increased cost in time or money.

Fig. 1-2: Consider these two ways of describing the same photo, which shows what "operation" adds to a model railroad: (1) Train 261, the *Florida Perishable* from the Virginian & Ohio, eases to a stop at SN Cabin in Sunrise, Va. The units will cut off so the Allegheny Midland switcher can add a "hot" load to its consist. (2) An imported brass MP15AC pauses with a plastic boxcar as three plastic diesels go by a kitbashed tower on an HO model railroad.

Increased realism

Realistic operation can greatly increase the overall realism of both your individual models and your model railroad as a whole. This is true even if you use ordinary, out-of-the-box models in a realistic and fascinating way to emulate the actions of full-size railroads. It's like an intense game of chess: After the game starts, you tend not to notice whether the rooks and knights are made of plastic or pewter or even sterling silver. Setting out a boxcar on a "hi-rail" Lionel O-27 layout requires the same moves and is therefore just as challenging and fun as on a finely scaled N or HO railroad (fig. 1-2).

Taking this analogy a step farther, one could enjoy a game of chess on a board drawn on a piece of cardboard with a felt-tip pen. Similarly, you can enjoy operation on an unscenicked or partially scenicked model railroad. Many modelers do just that for years—operation in and of itself really is that enjoyable! If you work

Fig. 1-3: Midland Road Mikado 639 on the Local North has set out carloads of kaolin and pulpwood on the Western Maryland interchange at North Durbin, W. Va. The WM's Mill Job will later switch the car into the Westvaco paper mill. Locating the mill on the WM instead of the AM thus added a job to each operating session. Moreover, having the freelanced AM interchange with a prototype railroad added believability to the AM by locating it in time and space.

toward completing key trackwork before finishing even one major area of scenery, you can start to enjoy the railroad much sooner. You can also spot the operational shortcomings before scenery makes it difficult to adjust the track arrangement.

Moreover, having a friend or two, or ten, stop by for regular operating sessions (once a month is common, but many railroads are operated almost every week) virtually ensures faster progress on the railroad. You want to show the crew that new industry you're kitbashing, so you hustle to get it done and installed on the layout for

Friday night's session. And you can bet that they'll pester you until you install that "missing" crossover needed for runaround moves in one of your towns. They'll probably offer to help build it!

How operation evolved

Operation evolved in step with the technical capabilities of our models. Just getting a locomotive running smoothly was once a major hurdle; today we can buy realistic ready-to-run locomotives that run like Swiss watches. Early car kits also took a lot of time to assemble and tune up, whereas today easy-to-build kits and even ready-to-use cars boast superb detail

and fidelity to prototype.

Early steps toward emulating railroad operation tended to focus on local or way freights where lots of the interesting switching action is. Locals stop at each town to switch industries, gathering "loose cars" and forwarding them to the next classification yard (fig. 1-3). There they are assembled into blocks for common destinations. The blocks are in turn assembled into trains headed to or toward that destination.

But locals are not the lifeblood of the railroad. Their work allows the stars of the show, money-making "through" and "fast" freights,

Fig. 1-4 (above): Virginian & Ohio fast-freight no. 262 behind an Appalachian Lines GP40 and an intermediate-scheme GP30 rounds the curve into Fullerton, Va., as it hustles auto parts to Atlanta and empty reefers back to Florida. The latter will soon return north loaded with produce on flip-side 261, the *Florida Perishable.* W. Allen McClelland photo

Fig. 1-5 (above right): Although the focus is usually on freight operations, passenger trains add both glamour and a sense of time-keeping to the railroad. Here Erie's no. 6, the *Lake Cities,* enters the curve at Cochecton, N.Y., behind a pair of Alco PA-1s on Harold Werthwein's HO Delaware Division, which is set in the early 1950s.

Fig. 1-6 (right): A model railroad can be an effective time machine carrying a modeler back to a favorite time and place. One magical moment was the steam era in the central Appalachians where massive Mallets worked the mine runs, then laid over at night—in this case at South Fork on the Allegheny Midland.

to thunder by on the main without having to make frequent stops to switch each and every town along the way. One of the first model railroads to put locals and freights into proper balance was Allen McClelland's highly regarded freelanced HO railroad, the Virginian & Ohio (fig. 1-4). His objective was for the V&O to be a well-defined segment of the continental rail transportation system. He succeeded so well that few of us regard the V&O as "freelanced."

As our knowledge has grown, and the time needed to get things running smoothly has dropped, operation has evolved to a remarkable degree. Many professional railroaders are also model railroaders, and their patient and gracious guidance has helped to foster the operational realism that is increasingly commonplace today.

A simulation

Think of operation not merely as a game but rather as a simulation of how a railroad works. It's about gathering individual freight cars, building blocks of cars headed for like destinations, then building trains from those blocks. It's about transferring cuts of cars between major railroad yards in cities. It's about an industrial engine or town switcher tending to a group of industries. It's about a branchline local or shortline freight puttering along a weed-grown

right-of-way in search of enough business to sustain it for yet another season.

I hasten to add that operation isn't just about freight trains, although the focus of most model railroads is on boxcars and hoppers rather than on coaches and sleepers. For those who appreciate the majesty of the passenger train, operation embraces putting together passenger and head-end (baggage, mail, and express) cars in a logical manner (fig. 1-5), dropping a diner here or picking up an extra coach or sleeper there,

perhaps even tacking some express or trailer-laden flatcars on the rear.

A time machine?

A model railroad that looks realistic and operates as well as or better than it looks is in essence a time machine that can take you back to a favorite era and locale (fig. 1-6). It's also a sophisticated simulator, much like the ones the pros use to learn how to control trains in various conditions. Operation can lead you to a keen understanding of how railroads and railroad-

Fig. 1-7: John King has carried the idea of replicating the work of professional railroaders to an amazing degree with his "model" of a dispatcher's office. All of the communications hardware is authentic. Paul Dolkos photo

Fig. 1-8: There's far more to operation than meets the eye. Here a V&O run-through caboose on train 262 passes a Midland Road caboose in the hole with the Local North at North Durbin, W. Va. Not seen but equally rewarding is the decades-long friendship between Allen McClelland, Steve King, and the author. The interactions of their merged Appalachian Lines railroads—the V&O, Virginia Midland, and AM—grew in tune with the friendship.

ers earn their living, and this in turn offers insights into the way the economy works now or worked in the past. In short, realistic operation involves making a series of knowledge-based business decisions, not merely playing a mindless game.

Yet we face no financial catastrophes or damaging train wrecks if we decide wrong, nor do we have to operate out in the rain or snow or in a mosquito-infested riverside yard on a steamy July evening. We do only the interesting, fun stuff and leave the really hard work to the professionals who, after all, get paid for their labors.

Modeling jobs

That said, operation is evolving toward "modeling jobs." We're discovering that what railroaders did or do for a living is often as fascinating to emulate as the train movements themselves. Some of us are therefore using slower fast-clock ratios, down from 8 or 6 to 1 to perhaps 3 or 2 or even 1 to 1, to allow time for, say, dispatchers to dictate train orders to operators in a captivatingly melodic cadence.

Modelers have traditionally assumed roles such as engineer, conductor, yardmaster, and dispatcher. With the increasing popularity of timetable and train-order operation, dispatchers are actually dictating train orders to one or more operators for delivery to train crews at locations specified on the orders (fig. 1-7). When not occupied with such duties, the operators also take on the role of traffic agents, just as their professional counterparts once did.

These agent-operators work with local crews to make real-time decisions about what customers need today, and what's ready to ship—rather than allowing preprinted waybills, be they filled out manually or computer-generated, to make all the go/no-go decisions. It's an exciting time to be a model railroader!

A social context

One last comment before we jump right into a "quick-start" operating session today with very little or no preparation time (Chapter 2): Operation has a social aspect as well. Many of my closest friends are fellow operators spread across the continent and indeed the planet (fig. 1-8). Many of my travels are occasioned by a distant operating session, and I invariably return home feeling that the time and money were well spent.

The National Model Railroad Association embraces a number of Special Interest Groups (SIGs), among them the Layout Design, Operations, and Signaling SIGs, which strongly focus on realistic operation. See section A-4 of the Appendix for contact information. So you're not alone in your quest to enjoy your railroad in new and rewarding ways. Once the word gets out that there's an operating layout nearby, you may suddenly meet new friends you never knew existed!

CHAPTER TWO

Quick-start guide to operation

Fig. 2-1: This view of Wingate, Ind., on the Nickel Plate Road's St. Louis Div. looks east past the depot. Note the vertically offset manual-block (not train-order) semaphores. The need to pick up train orders or messages was indicated by a red or yellow metal banner or lantern hung from a rung on the signal mast.

One thing's for sure about "operation": It's a lot more fun to do than to read about. I've therefore boiled down this entire book to one "quick-start" chapter to show you a simple but reasonably realistic way you can have an operating session—today!

I'll use a 4 x 8-foot model railroad depicting a small Indiana town called Wingate on the former New York, Chicago & St. Louis (Nickel Plate Road) as an example (fig. 2-1). You can adapt its lessons to a plan of virtually any size and scope.

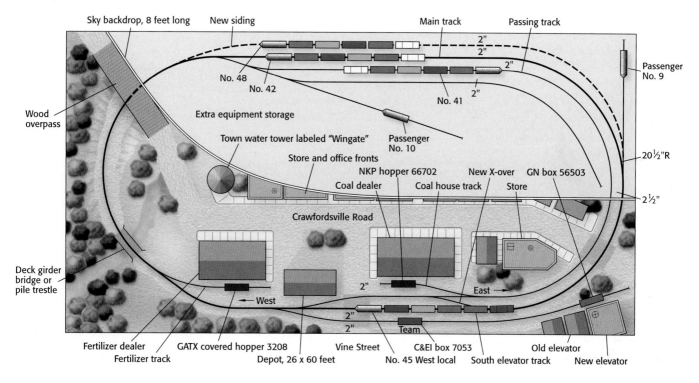

Sky backdrop, 8 feet long   New siding   Main track   Passing track

No. 48
No. 42
No. 41

2"
2"
2"
2"

Passenger No. 9

Wood overpass

Extra equipment storage

Town water tower labeled "Wingate"   Passenger No. 10

Store and office fronts

NKP hopper 66702   New X-over   GN box 56503

Coal dealer   Coal house track   Store

20½"R

2½"

Crawfordsville Road

Deck girder bridge or pile trestle

2"

East

← West

2"
2"

Team

Fertilizer dealer   GATX covered hopper 3208   Vine Street   C&EI box 7053   Old elevator
Fertilizer track   Depot, 26 x 60 feet   No. 45 West local   South elevator track   New elevator

The back portion of the plan (fig. 2-2) is shown as an unscenicked, hidden staging yard, but it could be a second modeled town used temporarily as staging yard. (For variety, you could use Wingate as the staging yard and the other town as the active area in the future.) As you'll learn later in this book, the goal is to find a way to suggest that trains go to and come from places beyond the confines of your railroad—"beyond the basement," as Allen McClelland put it.

More information on modeling Wingate appeared in the 1995 issue of Kalmbach's *Model Railroad Planning* annual (pages 50-57, "Small-town railroading, Midwest style"), and scale drawings of the Wingate depot appeared in March 1995 *Model Railroader* on pages 108-111. They're out of print, but you can obtain photocopies for a small fee by calling 1-800-533-6644.

If you already have a layout, focus on one town for this exercise. Later, you can use the information in this book to add sophistication, flexibility, and greater realism to the way cars are handled on your entire layout. The basic premise—simulate the function of a full-size railroad by moving cars and trains purposefully—won't change.

If you don't have a layout, you could quickly build this one using sectional track components in HO or N. The N scale version could have more staging tracks because of the closer track spacing. If you don't have room for a 4 x 8, we've also provided a linear version of this plan (fig. 2-3) you can quickly build on a shelf, perhaps atop a bookcase. Ask your local lumber dealer to saw a ⁵⁄₈" or ³⁄₄" 4 x 8-foot sheet of plywood in half lengthwise (two 2 x 8-foot pieces), then saw one of those halves into two 1 x 8-foot pieces. Each 1 x 8 piece is used as a hidden staging area to hold trains until they're needed on the scenicked 2 x 8 center section. You can "bend" this plan into an L or U shape to fit along two or three walls of a room by adding curved connector pieces to reach the staging yards.

Our objectives are simple: Use a system to move cars to and pick them up from the several industries in a small town. We also need to suggest that these cars came from somewhere else or are going to a more distant place, as the "foreign" railroad names on many of the freight cars indicate. In other words, why does a Great Northern boxcar appear on a railroad in Indiana?

One more objective: Have fun! You've spent time and money acquiring realistic models of full-size railroad equipment, and you've built a setting for them to run on. Now it's time to enjoy their utility as much as you enjoyed building and/or detailing them.

1 Locate your railroad on a map

You can't send a loaded car somewhere if you don't know which way it has to go to get there. If you're modeling a

Fig. 2-2: The town of Wingate, Ind., can be effectively modeled in HO on the front half of a 4 x 8-foot sheet. A crossover was added east of the depot to facilitate runaround moves. The rear of the layout is used for staging.

segment of a prototype railroad, as here (fig. 2-4), you already know that, say, east is to the right or counter-clockwise around your railroad. If you're freelancing, locating the railroad on a map of North America will help orient you. At least decide which way is east, preferably to your right so the "sun" (lighting) is to your back.

2 Name everything

It's no fun shipping a carload of beef to "the upper loop" or "back in the corner by the door." If you haven't done so already, assign place names to all "towns" and tracks within the towns on your railroad. This lets you route cars to specific places.

Major off-layout destinations or points of origin also

Wingate, Ind., Nickel Plate Road (Norfolk & Western)

Scale ³⁄₄" = 1'-0"

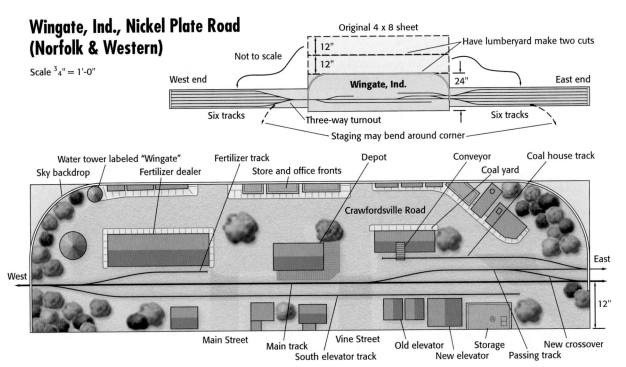

Fig. 2-3: The same 4 x 8-foot sheet can be cut into three pieces to make a 2 x 8 town scene and a pair of 1 x 8 staging or fiddle yards positioned to either side.

need names. This part of the Nickel Plate runs east from St. Louis through Wingate toward major eastern cities such as Toledo, Cleveland, and Buffalo. We can make trains on this tiny portion of the NKP seem to go to such distant places by using the back portion of the plan as a common east- and westbound staging yard. We'll think of it as "St. Louis" and "Frankfort."

3 Even east, odd west

We won't take time to create paperwork such as waybills, but we do need a scheme to cause cars to move in specific directions. Let's agree that any freight car that has a road number ending with an even digit (2, 4, 6, 8, or 0) will be sent east: even goes east. Any cars with road numbers that end in an odd digit (1, 3, 5, 7, 9) will be sent west. So Nickel Plate

Road boxcar 13567 would be routed west toward St. Louis, since 7 is odd.

Select from your roster enough freight cars to fill about 75 percent of the industry-track spots on the railroad. At Wingate, that's only three or four cars. Spot those cars at appropriate industries. Obviously, a stock car at a grain elevator or a tank car at a coal dealer might look odd, so make reasonable choices.

Now put a locomotive, four or more freight cars, and a caboose on the passing track to create a westbound local freight (also called a way freight, peddler, drill, and so on by other railroads).

4 Switching Wingate

Let's say that train no. 45, our West Local (trains get names and/or numbers too, although locals often operate as "extras"—more on that in Chapter 7), comprises four cars: ATSF and Monon boxcars, a loaded NKP hopper, and an NKP stock car. In town are GN box 56503 at the grain elevator, GATX covered hopper 3208 at the

fertilizer dealer, C&EI box 7053 on the team track, and NKP hopper 66702 sitting over the coal dealer's conveyor. Our local is headed west (to the left), so we'll pick up all westbound cars—those with odd last digits (GN and C&EI boxcars). An eastbound through freight (the NKP ran only a westbound local on this line) such as no. 42 or 48 can pick up the presumably empty GATX covered hopper and NKP hopper later today.

To keep things simple for this initial foray into operation, simply replace any car you pick up with a similar car, assuming one is in your train. The picked-up cars and any cars already in the local but not spotted go west with the local. We can replace the two boxcars with two from our train.

If the empty NKP hopper had an odd last digit and was thus going west by our convention, how would the West Local pick it up or spot a replacement hopper on the "facing-point" spur? On a model railroad, this requires a runaround move (fig. 2-5). I added a crossover in Wingate

to allow for runarounds. On the full-size NKP, train crews would get behind a car by doing a "drop," which is virtually impossible to do on a model railroad. What's a drop? Definitions of common operating terms appear in the Appendix.

The engine would stop its train clear of the crossover, uncouple an inbound hopper from the train, and leave it on the short runaround track in front of the coal dealer. It would then use the main to get behind (east of) the inbound hopper. It would pull east on the passing track, retrieve the outbound empty hopper, put it aside on the runaround, spot the inbound loaded hopper, then run around the outbound hopper to position the engine at its west end.

Now you know why switching areas usually include a runaround track! And if the main line through Wingate were really busy, you'd want a separate runaround track so the local could do most of its work without fouling the main.

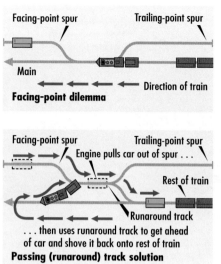

**THIRD SUBDIVISION
Clover Leaf District
St. Louis Division**

Facing-point dilemma

Passing (runaround) track solution

... then uses runaround track to get ahead
of car and shove it back onto rest of train

Fig. 2-4 (left): Modeling a segment of a prototype railroad, here the Third Subdivision of the NKP's St. Louis Div., or locating a freelanced railroad on a regional map helps to orient operators as they route cars and block trains. The map makes it easy to see that, for example, a car for St. Louis or beyond is routed to the west.

Fig. 2-5 (right): Trailing-point and facing-point moves.

work is done for today.

To increase running time (mileage), you may want to assign a number of laps for each train to run.

6 Do it over again!

It's quiet for a time in Wingate, but soon enough eastbound freight 48 eases into town and picks up eastbound cars—those with even last digits—which include the GATX covered hopper and NKP hopper. Picking up the covered hopper off the facing-point fertilizer spur will require running around.

If any other even-last-digit cars have since been spotted (perhaps the replacement cars the West Local switched out from its train or no. 42), you need to decide whether they have been loaded/unloaded. This is done by assuming the role of the NKP's agent-operator in Wingate, who typically works with the local crews to ensure that shippers' needs are met. (If your railroad has a lot of towns, you can see why the agent-operator's duties could be assigned to another crew member.)

5 Ready to leave town?

Switching accomplished and the West Local back together on the passing track, are we ready to head west? Let's wait in the clear at Wingate for no. 42, an eastbound through freight (eastbound and northbound trains are usually given even numbers). If it happens to have any cars for Wingate (an opportunity for you to make a logical decision about the needs of the business—your railroad and its customers), it could set them out on the runaround for the local to spot before it leaves town. It won't do any switching here, as the local is in the way. After 42 departs, the West Local handles any additional switching needs, perhaps takes a lunch break, then runs into the long stub-ended staging track, as its

7 Here comes no. 41!

While no. 48 is in town, through freight no. 41 rolls into view and perhaps makes a quick stop to set out a hot (important) car. It might be an empty boxcar or, in more modern times, covered hopper for the elevator during the wheat-rush season. No. 41 then continues one or more laps back into staging. No. 48 eventually finishes up its work and continues on east into staging.

If you utilize the two short stub-ended staging tracks to store gas-electrics or Budd RDCs, you could run passenger trains 9 and 10. (NKP trains 9 and 10 were powered by a single Alco PA-1, but there's not room for another pair of long staging tracks in HO unless you add an extension along the rear of the layout. In N scale, however, you'd be all set.) It will take a peek behind the backdrop to get the trains in and out of those spur tracks, but this increases the operating possibilities.

When your wristwatch says, for example, 7:30, it's time for any freight train or local in Wingate to clear up for no. 9, the westbound passenger train due at, say, 7:35. At 7:48, no. 10 is due through town. Maybe 9 and

10 occasionally meet in Wingate, complicating the picture for a freight train in town. It would have to duck into the team/elevator track or be gone prior to the meet.

8 Make adjustments and run it again

You can continue running the through freights and passenger trains, giving them new numbers: westbounds 43, 47, 49; and hot eastbounds 90, 96, and 98. Locals typically operate at most once a day, however, so at some point it's a good idea to simply terminate the session or declare it "tomorrow" and run a new sequence.

Looking ahead

By the time you've tired of the arbitrary nature of using odd and even last digits to determine direction, you'll have read through the rest of this book and have a head filled with more sophisticated ways to enhance your railroad's operation and your operating enjoyment.

By then, you'll also have learned that Wingate was probably a poor choice as a town to model, as it doesn't have an interchange with another railroad. You'll discover why that's important in the next chapter.

CHAPTER THREE

Basics of operation

Fig. 3-1: Livestock once moved primarily by rail. Laws governed the number of hours between feeding, watering, and exercising the critters. C. Bohi photo

Let's back up a step. To get you started, I've given you an overview of operation and some visual examples thereof (Chapter 1) and provided a Quick-Start Guide (Chapter 2) to let you try your hand at operation. But let's now review in greater detail our objectives in setting up realistic operating sessions on our railroads, then discuss the basics of operation on both prototype and model railroads.

Why railroads "operate"

The purpose of any business enterprise is to do work for a profit. To make this work manageable, railroads are divided into various departments. The mechanical department is responsible for locomotives and cars, for example, and the bridge and building folks take care of, well, bridges and buildings. The model railroad terms "operation" and "operating sessions" reflect the prototype's operating department, which keeps the railroad moving and, its management and investors hope, making money.

The bottom line is to move people or products efficiently from A to B. Both A and B are seldom on the same operating division or even the same railroad. (If the place where the product is shipped is quite close to the place where it's needed, it's typically trucked to the destination.) In fact, *neither* A nor B may be on the part of a railroad you've chosen to model.

On our model railroads, putting a cattle loading pen over here and a Swift packing plant over there may therefore not be a good idea. Better that we choose to model one or the other. Or we can simply participate in one leg of the journey of the bovines to their demise and neither originate nor terminate the shipment. You can model this "bridge traffic" by having a stock car appear from a staging yard at one end of your railroad, traverse the segment you've modeled as expeditiously as possible, and exit into a staging yard that simulates the next segment of your railroad or the railroad to which it connects.

We can enhance our part of the action by assuming that the livestock have been aboard the cramped quarters for close to 36 hours. Federal law requires livestock to be taken out of the car for rest, water, and feeding every 28 hours for at least five consecutive hours before reloading (fig. 3-1). (This time may be extended to 36 hours with customer authorization.) We can therefore model an intermediate exercise point and switch the cars to be unloaded and then reloaded there. This can actually be specified on the waybill accompanying that car. So we didn't actually lose much by not modeling either the cattle-loading pens or the meat packing plant, did we?

You'll find repeated references in this book to

Fig. 3-2: Imagine the car-movement possibilities: An interchange is located at almost every point where the lines cross on this simplified map of the Illinois rail network.

Fig. 3-3: It's hard to fathom that 12,000 loads (and an equal number of empties) were interchanged annually at Humrick, Ill., a remote crossing between the Nickel Plate's St. Louis line and the Milwaukee's Southeastern line to southern Indiana. That's an average of 66 cars per day, so frequent pick-ups from the interchange track (left of train) were obviously paramount. Chris Manthey photo

Fig. 3-4: The shortline Ridgeley & Midland County (right), which connected to the Allegheny Midland at South Fork, W. Va., offered a less hectic respite for crew members than working an AM road job. The Ten Wheeler belongs to Max Robin. Short lines were also home to older and more exotic motive power such as these Baldwin AS-416s on the original Norfolk Southern (below) in December 1972.

interchanges between railroads that cross at grade. That's because interchanges are a major source of traffic, especially in the central states and provinces where railroads form a clearly visible network (see Illinois map: fig. 3-2). Few loads both originate and terminate on the same railroad. Rather, they are received from and/or given to a connecting "foreign" railroad at interchange points (fig. 3-3).

Operating objectives

The idea of participating in some aspect of the manner in which cars are forwarded is what we call operation. Just as in the previous example where stockcars were moved with a specific destination in mind, every other type of car

can similarly be moved purposefully. No space for a refinery? You can still move tank cars by bringing them out of a staging track that represents a route from the refinery to your railroad, running them over the segment of the rail network your railroad represents, and then allowing them to disappear into another staging yard. A few tank cars may actually stop at destinations on your railroad, such as a local fuel dealer, depending on the era your railroad depicts.

Start to think of every loaded car on your railroad as a container filled with something needed elsewhere. Where did it come from? What does it contain? Where is it going? When does it need to be there?

How can you make that happen?

But why delve into such elaborate plots? Doesn't trying to adhere to a schedule and switching cars to specified locations cause a lot of stress? Isn't a hobby about getting rid of stress?

Seeking a balance

Consider this: As colorfully described by Fred Frailey in the August 2002 *Trains* Magazine, a brand-spanking-new, 17-year-old Texas & Pacific operator named Newell Derryberry was so alarmed by the need to copy a train order for the onrushing Fruit Block that he completely forgot railroad Morse code and had to take the order over a static-filled telephone line. Then Derryberry was so cowed by the sight of the train bearing down on him that he stood too far back for the outstretched arm of a brakeman to snag the orders Derryberry was holding up on his "hoop." Exciting, eh?

Maybe it's a little too exciting for a hobby context. A good challenge can be fun and instructional, but I don't like a lot of knuckle-whitening pressure. One can make anything stressful if he

or she approaches it the wrong way, however. So we need to find a balance that fosters challenge and entertainment without creating undue pressure. Just don't give up too quickly.

Never built a resin freight car kit? You'll probably experience some stress the first time you put one together. After that, they get a lot easier. Never soldered before? You'll experience some stress when you discover that hot solder invariably falls where it can do you the most harm. Next time, you'll be wiser.

Operation can also become stressful if you lose sight of the objectives. You're not trying to win a contest where the first one across the finish line gets a ribbon. Rather, you're trying to use a miniature railroad to simulate the movement of products and people over a segment of a transportation system. If that segment is a part of the Northeast Corridor or any other busy piece of railroad, veteran operators may relish the challenge, but the newcomer is going to sweat rivets. So be careful what you wish for.

Operation, like model railroading, is very broad-shouldered. There are so many

Fig. 3-5 (left): Allegheny Midland train 261, the *Florida Perishable,* eases to a stop at Big Springs Jct., W. Va., to set air brake retainers before descending treacherous Cheat River Grade. Only an hour earlier, the train had been handed off to the AM by the Virginian & Ohio.

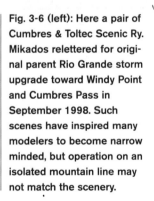

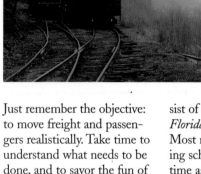

Fig. 3-6 (left): Here a pair of Cumbres & Toltec Scenic Ry. Mikados relettered for original parent Rio Grande storm upgrade toward Windy Point and Cumbres Pass in September 1998. Such scenes have inspired many modelers to become narrow minded, but operation on an isolated mountain line may not match the scenery.

Fig. 3-7 (right): Shortline mountain railroads such as the Graham County couldn't exist without a connection to the continental rail network. This May 1974 photo shows the Southern Ry. interchange with the GC at Graham County Jct. in North Carolina. The GC could be staged as an SR interchange, or the SR could be a staged connection to the short line, which only weeks before had used a Shay instead of a GE 70-tonner.

aspects of operation that surely one or more of them will prove rewarding to you. One of the best-known operators in the U.S. once visited my model railroad and instantly gravitated to a connecting short line (fig. 3-4). He felt the Allegheny Midland's busy main line was too intimidating for a first-time visitor. Other first-timers dived right in, how-

ever, eager to test their mettle against the demands of a hectic schedule.

To each his or her own, but if you ease into this thing called operation, you're far more apt to like what you find there. You do have to get your feet wet, however.

Just remember the objective: to move freight and passengers realistically. Take time to understand what needs to be done, and to savor the fun of doing it as a professional railroader would approach the same task.

Not sure what a pro would do? Then think through the business implications of what needs to be done and make a reasonable decision. Again, it's not a game with invented rules. You're simulating how a full-size railroad would approach its business needs.

What's too fast?

Railroads run by the clock, as their customers do. If those refrigerator cars being loaded with fruit aren't ready for pick-up by 5:00 p.m., for example, there won't be time to switch them into the con-

sist of today's *Fruit Block* or *Florida Perishable* (fig. 3-5). Most model railroad operating schemes therefore use time as a benchmark to gauge progress.

A main tool of operation is the fast-time clock, which typically runs anywhere from twice as fast as a normal clock to perhaps 12 times that rate. The increased clock speed makes it seem as though our railroads are longer, as more time elapses between the start and end of each movement. (We'll look more closely at clock ratios in Chapter 7.)

Such clocks can also be the main culprit when it comes to adding undue tension to an operating session, so caution is advised. In fact, an increasing number of highly experienced operators are

Fig. 3-9: A truncated main and interchange track suffice to create an interchange on a narrow oNeTRAK module. Spotting a dummy foreign-road locomotive or caboose nearby could establish the identity of the crossing railroad. Bernie Kempinski photo

Truncated Interchange

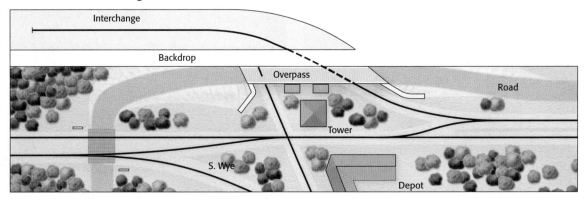

Interchange

Backdrop

Overpass

Road

Tower

S. Wye

Depot

Aisle

slowing down the ratios of their fast-clocks or using regular 1:1 clocks. They could handle basic train movements at the fast pace, but now they want to allow time to enjoy doing the myriad things that operation embodies: writing and reading train orders, perhaps, or having time to do yard and local switching moves without overheating the tires of their locomotives and the space between their ears.

If you feel a little tension, fine; that goes with learning a new set of procedures. Learning to fly an airplane causes some tension, but for most fledgling pilots the rewards of flying make the investment worthwhile. Similarly—and this is a very important point—operation is worth some effort to mas-

ter, as it offers a lifetime of model railroading enjoyment.

Consider the alternative: You spend a lot of time and effort, and not an insignificant amount of money, building a layout. You get it as done as a model railroad ever gets, and you run some trains around it. By about the tenth lap around the new railroad, a sameness sets in. Is this it? Typically, this is where a layout begins to acquire a patina of dust. Soon, it's dismantled, and you start building a New & Improved layout. Several years later, you're still building—your fifth, or maybe eighth, layout. If your primary enjoyment in the hobby is derived from building layouts, this is fine.

But if what you really want is to enjoy the model railroad

once it's built, realistic operation can go a long way toward meeting that goal while keeping you entertained along the way. By superimposing operation—it's better to design a railroad to support realistic operation from the get-go, but it can be overlaid on most existing layouts—driving the gold spike is just a milestone along a longer road, one that offers a new kind of reward at each step of the way. At very little additional cost, literally years and years of enjoyment are accorded the devotee of operation.

Railroading as we like it

Most of us have a favorite railroad or two, or at least a type of railroading we admire. Often as not, it's the hometown railroad we grew

Fig. 3-8: A crossing-at-grade with another railroad and the usual leg-of-a-way interchange track can be modeled on a narrow shelf. If there's room behind the backdrop, the interchange track can be extended to accommodate considerably more traffic.

up with. In other cases, a trip to, say, Colorado to ride one of the former Rio Grande narrow-gauge lines triggers a desire to replicate in miniature a piece of what we saw there (fig. 3-6). Maybe we were oblivious to railroading until we received a train set from Christmas or spotted one running in a hobby shop window or a bank lobby around the holidays.

Most any type of railroading can be modeled successfully, including its operation.

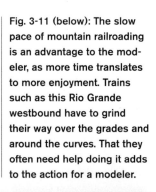

Fig. 3-10 (left): Mountain railroads such as the Louisville & Nashville (CSX today) usually followed steep-sided river valleys. An eastbound out of Corbin, Ky., in April 1974 navigates through the central Appalachians, where crossings at grade with other railroads are rare.

Fig. 3-11 (below): The slow pace of mountain railroading is an advantage to the modeler, as more time translates to more enjoyment. Trains such as this Rio Grande westbound have to grind their way over the grades and around the curves. That they often need help doing it adds to the action for a modeler.

It's also true that some railroads are more interesting to watch at work than others, and this translates to the model with equal ease. The main point to keep in mind is that great-looking equipment and scenery do not necessarily translate to great operation.

A one-horse short line may have the most appealing teakettle up front one could hope to model, but it does nothing more than plod up and down what passes for a short main line once a day with cars from a mill destined for an interchange with a more prosperous mainline railroad (fig. 3-7). Fun to model? You bet! Fun to operate? Probably not.

A solution: Model enough of the big-time railroad that interchanges with the short line to add some action. One town, if it has enough industry, might do it. The short line makes the mill run and lays over waiting for the larger railroad's local to show up. The local arrives, switches the interchange and several local industries, then waits till a scheduled passenger train glides into town, makes its stop, and leaves. The local then finishes up its work and departs. Finally, the shortline crew gathers the inbound empties for the mill and heads for home.

The interchange between the short line and the trunk-line railroad is one illustration of a key facet of most model railroad designs. Interchanges are among the most versatile and productive lengths of track you can model. These "universal industries" are also highly efficient in that they consume little layout area—there's no space-eating "factory" (fig. 3-8)—and most of

Fig. 3-12: Before this Atlantic Great Eastern train (left) could assault the hill, it had to stop at the foot of the grade, drop its caboose, and have a pusher slide into the gap. Shoving on a wood caboose that didn't have a steel underframe was forbidden on some lines. Steel cabooses could stand the compressive forces, as the Western Maryland demonstrated (right) on Williamsport Hill near Hagerstown, Md., in May 1974.

Coal Deposits in the United States

Anthracite
Bituminous
Subbituminous, lignite, brown coal

their length can be in hidden staging (fig. 3-9). Because the interchanged traffic is often "hot" and has to be kept moving, it's often set out and picked up by through freights rather than once-a-day locals. A huge variety of car types and quantities, no structures to build, and a sense of urgency place interchanges at the very top of the must-have list for many model railroads.

Mountain railroading

In the mountains where railroads are forced to follow narrow river valleys, there is scenery in abundance but seldom interchange at grade with a crossing foreign road (fig. 3-10). Instead, the railroads tend to connect end-to-end and interchange virtually entire trains. This was especially true before the recent spate of mergers—the Western Pacific essentially being a continuation of the Denver & Rio Grande via

Salt Lake City, Utah, for example. (Both are part of the Union Pacific today.)

The lack of along-the-line interchanges is a concern for those who choose to model a mountain railroad. An offsetting factor is that mountain railroads often operate more slowly (fig. 3-11), thus extending the running time over a division. This has the effect of lengthening our always-too-short model railroads. Moreover, mountain grades usually require the use of helper or pusher engines (fig. 3-12), which adds to the running time and interest.

Transfer runs

In large cities, railroads effect car interchange via transfer runs between major yards (fig. 3-13). An increasingly popular approach to layout design is to model several rail yards in one metropolitan area and have crews spend the entire operating session switching, then mov-

ing cars between yards. Main lines are typically downplayed or not even modeled. Jim Senese's Kansas City Terminal (fig. 3-14) is a fine example of this trend.

The crews thus get a mixture of yard switching and transfer runs to maintain their interest for several hours. The variety is endless: When they return from a transfer run to one railroad, they discover that while they were gone another crew has brought them a new cut of cars to switch.

Union operating agreements often required that a transfer run from the AB&C to the XY&Z could deliver cars only, then go back "light" (engine only) or as a "caboose hop" (engine and caboose). The XY&Z's crews

would handle deliveries to the AB&C. This creates more variety and extra jobs on a model railroad.

What goes where, and when?

Knowing what might be lurking inside the plastic shell of that Santa Fe boxcar requires some knowledge of what railroads shipped, from where, to where, and when. A basic understanding of the regional distribution of many products is especially helpful for the freelancer as he or she tries to establish a regionally plausible industrial base for the railroad. The map shown in fig. 3-15 provides some insights into the North American distribution of coal. A visit to the library's geography section will lead you to similar maps for oil, agricultural products, chemicals, forest products, paper, auto production, iron ore, and so on. I even found one showing the distribution of farm tractors throughout the U.S. in 1954!

A freelanced model railroad called the North Dakota Eastern would therefore be expected to move a lot of

Fig. 3-16 (left): The Virginian & Ohio has been set in a succession of eras, and evidence of its past isn't hard to find. Note that the second Alco Century 424 of this westbound manifest has yet to be repainted in the post-1968 Appalachian Lines scheme worn by the lead unit.
W. Allen McClelland photo

grain. The West Virginian would be a major coal hauler. The New England & Southern would haul potatoes as well as paper and forest products. The Oregon & Northern could be another lumber line. The Texas & Missouri would benefit from petroleum products, while the Southeast Coast Ry. would forward a lot of reefers to northern cities.

Full-size railroads often bragged about their traffic base. The Delaware, Lackawanna & Western was "The Road of Anthracite." Not many railroads could make such a boast, since this hard coal mining was largely confined to northeastern Pennsylvania. Others bragged about their passenger trains: The names of Santa Fe's famous fleet were billboarded on their boxcars. Some wanted us to know where they went: Burlington painted "Everywhere West" on their boxcars. UP insisted it could handle it.

Such slogans make it easier for the prototype modeler to understand the management philosophy of the railroad he or she has opted to model,

but the freelancer should consider making such determinations up front. A small layout, be it prototype or freelanced, can realistically accommodate a large passenger fleet only if it has adequate staging and focuses on operations at one busy locale, such as a junction where trains split to serve two destinations.

Locating your railroad in time

Railroading has changed dramatically over the years. Thanks to a wide and growing variety of products, it's not difficult to model a wide range of notable eras. The hard part is deciding which one to model.

A few modelers have attempted, with some success, to model more than one era, but not at the same time (fig. 3-16). By carefully choosing lineside structures or by making time-specific structures removable, different eras can be represented. It's hard enough to become familiar with the equipment, architecture, and operating practices of a single major era, however, so approach such grandiose have-your-cake-and-eat-it-too schemes with caution.

The steam-to-diesel transition era of the 1940s to 1960 remains among the most popular eras to model. Until recently, a good variety of smooth-running, affordable steam models wasn't available, so modelers had but a few token steam locomotives and let inexpensive diesels shoulder the bulk of the work.

Be sure that key locomotives are available and affordable, and that they perform as well as you expect or your railroad's operating scheme requires. A diminutive 4-4-0 that hung on into the '40s or '50s may look appealing, but it may not pull more than a car or two up the spiral helix leading from hidden staging to the rest of the railroad.

Fig. 3-17: This bit of "texture" from the steam era survived, but just barely, into 1974 as the L&N itself closed out a noble career before joining the Family Lines and then CSX. It's increasingly hard to find depots, water towers, coal docks, roundhouses, turntables, and other such relics of the age of steam on full-size railroads, but they're alive and well on numerous model railroads.

Texture

"Texture" is a term Dave Frary uses to suggest that there are things we can do to make our models more appealing. A plastic house or depot kit gains texture when details such as gutters,

Fig. 3-18 (right): The Alphabet Route originally extended from Ohio and ran east via the Wheeling & Lake Erie (later NKP), Pittsburgh & West Virginia, Western Maryland, Reading, and Central Railroad of New Jersey. Here's evidence of run-through power in the form of second-generation Reading units teaming up with first-generation WM Fs to hustle freight through eastern Pennsylvania in May 1974. The months following a merger also produce lash-ups with a jumble of pre-merger paint schemes.

Fig. 3-19 (left): Modeling a branch of a large railroad offers a nice mix of the attributes of a large railroad with those of a short line. Here the N&W's Abingdon Branch local to West Jefferson, N.C., rounds the bend at Green Cove, a place memorialized by the late O. Winston Link in *The Last Steam Railroad in America*. Operation on such lines may be limited, however; only one train worked this branch.

downspouts, electric meters, open doors and windows, broken siding, missing shingles, and weathering are added. Similarly, a railroad gains texture when the various appurtenances found at lineside are modeled.

This is what contributes to the popularity of the steam era. Each town typically had a depot (fig. 3-17). Many towns sported a water tower, as steam locomotives were notoriously thirsty beasts. Branch lines often used small steam power that fit on short turntables, prompting the use of short tenders and in turn more frequent stops for water and perhaps coal.

Brakemen had to climb atop moving cars to set brakes or retainers, so tell-tales—hanging ropes or wires—were located to warn them they were approaching a low clearance such as an overhead bridge. Small industries such as coal yards, local fuel dealers, lumber yards, stock pens, team tracks, unloading ramps for farm implements and automobiles, and so on graced many communities that today warrant little more than a wave from the cab to waiting motorists.

Such texture extends to operation. A stop for water may require the train to be brought to a halt, the steam engine cut off and run up to the water tank or column (free-standing pipe with spout), the engine returned to the train, and the air brakes pumped off. If there is one or more helper engines, the process is repeated. Pushers cut in mid-train or at the rear? Imagine the difficulty of coordinating the watering of iron horses perhaps a mile apart using only whistle signals, subtle changes on air-pressure gauges, and years of hard-won experience!

The myriad local industries along a division kept local crews busy. Today, the local may work fewer but larger customers, perhaps grouped in an industrial park, so there is no lack of switching even in more modern times.

Mergers and power pools

Railroads have always grown by merging with other lines, but today the number of large railroads is down to a handful. The days when someone modeling the Pacific Northwest could choose between a partially electrified Milwaukee Road plus the likes of the Great Northern, the Northern Pacific, and the Spokane, Portland & Seattle are gone. So is the successor Burlington Northern, itself part of Burlington Northern Santa Fe.

Elsewhere, it's the Union Pacific, Kansas City Southern, CSX, or Norfolk Southern. Period. Even once-mighty Conrail, like its predecessors (fig. 3-18), is now a fallen flag. Fortunately for variety's sake, regional and shortline railroads are flourishing where the big-time railroads couldn't afford to compete due to labor agreements and other elements of their cost structure. For the modeler, this opens up opportunities: Model a very small part of a large railroad or, percentage-wise, a much larger

Fig. 3-20 (above): The Western Maryland switches the Westvaco paper mill as Allegheny Midland Alco RS-11s power AJN-1, an Alpha Jet, through North Durbin, W. Va. Modeling a part of the WM's Elkins line created jobs for WM crews and tied the freelanced AM to a well-known regional prototype in a specific era.

part of a small railroad. It may be two or three towns, but that could allow all or most of the signature locations along a short line or a regional railroad to be modeled.

If you want to model a large railroad but keep the scope of the project within more modest boundaries, seek out a branch line (fig. 3-19). They offer many of the same opportunities as a short line—older power, lighter rail, more "texture," and a less-hectic pace.

Trackage rights also create opportunities for operational variety. On the Allegheny Midland, for example, I modeled a section of the Western Maryland's Elkins line (fig. 3-20). The AM had trackage rights over the WM from Glady (an actual

place) to North Durbin (a mythical town near Durbin, W. Va.—see fig. 1-3). Advantages included tying the AM to a prototype railroad with its known home region and era-specific paint schemes and creating more jobs (WM crews switched town industries).

The AM also pooled power with merger partners Virginian & Ohio (Allen McClelland—see fig. 3-21)

and Virginia Midland (Steve King). Prior to the AM-V&O-VM merger into the Appalachian Lines in 1968, the AM pooled power with owner Nickel Plate Road (fig. 3-22). This allowed me to freelance without venturing too far into the land of Anything Goes. I dubbed this "prototype freelancing," an imperfect term that has nonetheless become part of the hobby's lingo. The impact

Fig. 3-21: Model railroads can merge too. McClelland's V&O, King's Virginia Midland, and Koester's AM "merged" in 1968 to form the Appalachian Lines, which made cooperative operations such as run-through power and cabooses even more deeply entrenched.

Fig. 3-22: Until 1964, the Nickel Plate Road had a controlling interest in the Midland Road, as was evident from its choices of motive power and paint scheme. Here a trio of Alco RSD-12s chugs by the division offices at South Fork, W. Va., on the point of yet another Great Lakes-bound coal drag.

Fig. 3-23: By looking at the consist, operators should be able to identify many trains. The Lehigh Valley and Pittsburgh & Lake Erie boxcars and P&LE caboose mark this train as SR-12 out of Connellsville, Pa., rather than AJS-12 off the Norfolk & Western (NKP) at Dillonvale, O. The latter would be expected to have more cars from midwestern and western lines.

orchestrate with four-cycle waybills (Chapter 6).

Terminology and names

Nothing adds more realism to an operating session than the correct use of terminology, be it the wording in a train order or an instruction communicated by radio. "Engine 456 run extra Danville to Grange" or "Spot the Burlington boxcar at the beer distributor, then head up the running track to Mill Street, over" sound the same on a railroad of any size. By using proper terminology, you can operate on a railroad comprising sectional track nailed down to a sheet of plywood and still have a really good time. (Been there, done that!)

on operation is that trains with pooled power were often those that had hotter schedules, as engine changes at terminals were avoided.

Such visual clues and cues help operators know at a glance what train is headed their way and how to regard it. In a professional railroading environment where the same thing happens at about the same time day after day, and the same people do the same jobs, the need for

visual crutches is lessened. But on a model railroad where we operate once a month, we need all the visual aids we can get.

That extends to car types in the train. A train with a lot of cars from New England railroads offers different identity clues than one with midwestern cars. On the Allegheny Midland, one could tell train AJN-1, which connected with the Nickel Plate's AJ-1 in Ohio, from

CV-1, which went to Connellsville, Pa., merely by noting the consist: AJN-1 had a lot of midwestern cars (Chicago & North Western, Soo Line, Milwaukee Road, Grand Trunk Western, Monon, NKP, etc.), whereas northbound CV-1 and "flipside" (southbound) SR-12 invariably had eastern cars such as Pittsburgh & Lake Erie, Delaware & Hudson, Reading, and Lehigh Valley (fig. 3-23). This was easy to

Fig. 3-24: No doubt about it: This is Mt. Carbon on the C&O in West Virginia (right). The use of signs on posts or depots helps crews to know where they are at all times, a key aspect of realistic operations. Print some signs (below right) on your laser printer, glue them to strips of wood or styrene, add border frames and posts, and you're in business.

Using proper terminology and names is critical on a full-size railroad. The dispatcher may issue a train order for a westbound train to "take siding" (enter the passing track) to meet an eastbound train, so train crews need to know which track is which. There could be an east passing track and a west passing track on either side of the depot. A mistake could be costly if either train passed the proper siding just as the opposing train arrived. A customer would surely be upset if a carload of lumber were left at the grain elevator.

All tracks and all locations should therefore be named (fig. 3-24). A car isn't spotted (moved to and left at) the track "over by the elevator" or "under the basement stairs" but on the elevator track. Trains don't meet over by the door but at Wingate. Clearance is not issued to the track under the overpass but to the west switch at Charleston.

The "west" switch? Directions are established by defining east or north to the right, for example. When railroads operated by timetables and train orders, east- and northbound trains were

usually superior by direction to west- and southbound trains. Names and directions are therefore critical to safe and efficient operation.

A train is a locomotive, with or without cars displaying markers, which are lanterns or flags hung on the end of the locomotive or the last car in the train. Today, a flashing rear-end device indicates the end of a train. A main point to understand in terms of operation is that a helper engine coasting back down a hill after shoving a train to the summit itself becomes a train for dispatching purposes. No cars, no caboose—but it's still a train if it has markers.

Other common railroad terms that pertain to operation are explained in the Appendix at the rear of this book. The Appendix also contains AAR designations for basic freight car types. The passenger car section shows the typical door and window arrangements of common types of "varnish," a term left over from the days when wooden passenger cars wore a gleaming coat of varnish.

Tough decisions

Choosing an era to depict is among the more difficult choices you need to make. Railroads and railroading have changed dramatically, especially in recent years. "Traditional" railroad institutions such as the roundhouse, turntable, coal dock, water tower, and even the depot and caboose are largely consigned to the pages of history.

Does the drama of an approaching SD70M or AC4400 offset this loss? That's for you to decide. But think of such attributes in terms of modeling them, and then operating the models. Modern locomotives and cars and trains are typically

quite long, and a freight racing across the prairies with nary a stop doesn't offer much operational variety. Is there a local or mine run on this line that ups the ante? Are helpers added just ahead? Does this train stop at an important interchange or industry to make critical pick ups or set outs?

The key is not so much what era and railroad you choose to model but how you choose to model it. If you pick a segment of your favorite prototype or base prototype that is as much fun to run as it is to model, you'll never run out of creative ways to spend your hobby time.

CHAPTER FOUR

Classification and staging yards

Fig. 4-1: The compact yard at Midland was a bit too small for use as a division-point yard where locals originated, so it was renamed South Fork and primarily used as a home for mine shifters. A B&O local, staged on a leg of the wye as the session began, delivered coal and picked up empties from the interchange track between the Mikado and the Railroad YMCA crew hotel.

A detailed discussion of classification and staging (or fiddle) yard operation could alone fill this book. A brief overview of yard and engine terminal design should help you avoid the most common pitfalls that detract from realistic operation, however.

If you're still in the design stage, remember that yards can take up a lot of space. You therefore face some hard-nosed decisions about whether you actually need one or more division-point yards.

Fig. 4-2 (above): The Western Maryland's yard at Elkins, W. Va., primarily gathered coal from branch mines and allocated empty hoppers to mine runs. It also repaired the hopper fleet on the tracks at right. The substantial brick depot is at far left, and the roundhouse was located across the tracks to its right.

Fig. 4-3 (above right): You get two for the price of one at the Clinchfield-C&O yard at Elkhorn City, Ky.—a small yard and a major industry in the form of a series of coal tipples crammed between the Big Sandy River and the mountainside. Note the CRR's Santa Fe-style steel caboose at left.

When I designed the Allegheny Midland, I decided that I needed two division-point yards, one at Sunrise, Va., the other at Midland, W. Va. But the lack of space at Midland precluded a yard with tracks sufficiently long to handle typical 25- to 30-car trains. Jim Boyd suggested using the Midland yard as a coal yard that mine shifters worked out of and renaming it South Fork (fig. 4-1). The division point was then moved into the north-end staging yard, which was renamed North Yard at Midland.

The down side, and there always is one, of this change was that Appalachia Division crews no longer got on and off their trains in a modeled engine terminal. As I'll explain shortly, I was close to resolving that concern when the railroad was abandoned.

Prototype yards need not be huge, especially if they are, like South Fork, limited in scope. The Western Maryland's coal-marshalling yard at Elkins, W. Va., is an example of a modest-size yard (fig. 4-2). Only modest amounts of merchandise freight were handled through here. Elkhorn City, Ky., where the C&O's Big Sandy line met the Clinchfield (fig. 4-3), was another modest facility, and it had a bonus: Numerous coal tipples were located right along the east side of the yard.

Perhaps you can instead combine a visible classification yard with a partially hidden staging yard, with one yard doing the work of two. I was converting the Allegheny Midland's hidden north-end staging yard into a partially visible yard (fig. 4-4) when I decided it was time to start over on a new layout, but the idea was a good one. Allen McClelland made a similar change to the Virginian & Ohio's formerly hidden west-end staging yard (fig. 4-5), as he described in the 1998

issue of *Model Railroad Planning.*

Yard operation

To illustrate a basic yard, we've reprinted Andy Sperandeo's well-thought-out plan for an N scale division-point yard (fig. 4-6) from the July 2002 *Model Railroader.* It's fed on either end by a staging yard, but it could just as easily have a long mainline run at one end.

I don't recommend putting a modeled main line at both ends of this or any other

Fig. 4-4: The original design for the entry into north-end staging on the Allegheny Midland was via the road underpass next to the American-Standard factory (above, center). Access was via a panel at right. As that yard evolved into a combination classification and staging yard, the throat was daylighted (above), which provided better road crew access to their trains and more space for industries and a freight house (in mock-up form), as this under-construction photo shows.

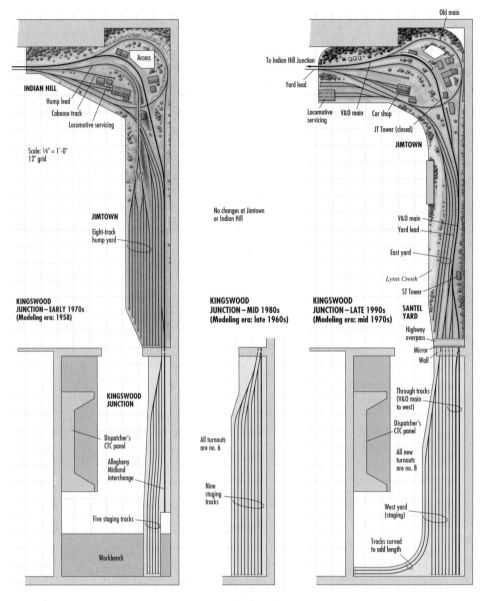

Old main

To Indian Hill Junction

Yard lead

INDIAN HILL

Hump lead

Caboose track

Locomotive servicing

Locomotive servicing

V&O main

Car shop

JT Tower (closed)

Scale: ¼" = 1'-0"
12" grid

JIMTOWN

Eight-track hump yard

No changes at Jimtown or Indian Hill

JIMTOWN

V&O main

Yard lead

East yard

Lynn Creek

ST Tower

SANTEL YARD

Highway overpass

Mirror Wall

KINGSWOOD JUNCTION – EARLY 1970s
(Modeling era: 1958)

KINGSWOOD JUNCTION – MID 1980s
(Modeling era: late 1960s)

KINGSWOOD JUNCTION – LATE 1990s
(Modeling era: mid 1970s)

KINGSWOOD JUNCTION

Dispatcher's CTC panel

Allegheny Midland interchange

All turnouts are no. 6

Through tracks (V&O main to west)

Dispatcher's CTC panel

All new turnouts are no. 8

Nine staging tracks

Five staging tracks

West yard (staging)

Workbench

Tracks curved to add length

modeled yard, however, as locating a yard in the center of your main line cuts the run in half (fig. 4-7). It's usually better to put the yard next to a staging or fiddle yard that simulates the next division to the east or west, or north or south. The crew member who acts as the engine hostler, servicing and turning locomotives between runs, can also serve as the crew for all trains entering and leaving the adjacent staged division.

The key elements of good yard design are evident in Andy's plan. On the right end is a drill track, also known as a yard lead, with a crossover near the ladder to allow arriving and departing trains to enter or leave the yard from the main. Some of the yard tracks are double-ended, nicely serving as arrival/departure tracks, while others are stub-ended to maximize their length. The yard engine can build a train in the stub tracks, then move it over to a double-ended track and add a caboose prior to departure.

The caboose track can easily be reached from the lead. And although engines cutting off from inbound freights or heading out to couple onto outbound freights block the yard goat's work, they do so for only a few moments.

A freight house and team track are located nearby for customers who don't have their own sidings. Andy also

Fig. 4-5: Allen McClelland extended his west-end staging yard by projecting it through the wall of the dispatcher's office, then detailed the east end of the yard. This replaced a hump yard on the original plan. A mirror above the highway overpass disguises the wall. W. Allen McClelland photo

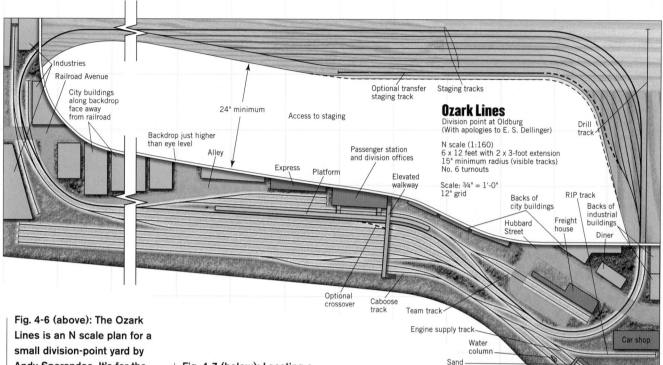

Industries
Railroad Avenue
City buildings along backdrop face away from railroad
24" minimum
Access to staging
Optional transfer staging track
Staging tracks
Backdrop just higher than eye level
Alley
Express
Platform
Passenger station and division offices
Elevated walkway
Drill track

Ozark Lines
Division point at Oldburg
(With apologies to E. S. Dellinger)

N scale (1:160)
6 x 12 feet with 2 x 3-foot extension
15" minimum radius (visible tracks)
No. 6 turnouts

Scale: ¾" = 1'-0"
12" grid

Backs of city buildings
RIP track
Backs of industrial buildings
Hubbard Street
Freight house
Diner
Car shop

Optional crossover
Caboose track
Team track
Engine supply track
Water column
Sand
Coal
Ashes
120-foot turntable (Walthers 933-32030)
Crew room and roundhouse office
Six-stall roundhouse (Walthers 933-3202)

Fig. 4-6 (above): The Ozark Lines is an N scale plan for a small division-point yard by Andy Sperandeo. It's for the modeler who primarily enjoys the challenges of efficiently switching a yard while accommodating inbound and outbound trains. It also features a sizable passenger station.

Fig. 4-7 (below): Locating a major yard in the middle of the railroad shortens mainline runs in both directions. Locating the yard next to staging at one end of the railroad maximizes the mainline run.

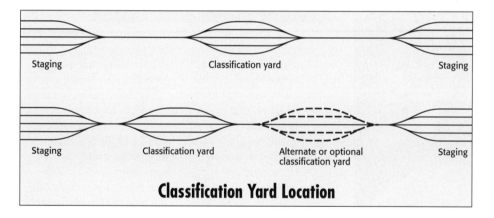

Staging
Classification yard
Staging

Staging
Classification yard
Alternate or optional classification yard
Staging

Classification Yard Location

provided a modicum of passenger-train operating potential: Note the substantial passenger station and nearby express tracks. A post office could also be located here where Railway Post Office cars are loaded and unloaded.

The car shop and RIP (repair-in-place) track are actually sources of traffic in that cars can be moved to and from this track during an operating session. At least

one carload of sand and coal can be spotted on the engine-supply track, and an outbound load of cinders will need to be moved each day. There are also a few local industries for the yard crew or an "industrial engine" to switch.

Working a yard

Think of a yard as a series of pigeonholes into which cars are sorted like letters at

the post office. All of the letters for, say, Elm Street or Rural Delivery Route 1 are sorted into one slot, just as all of the cars for the local are sorted into one track. Once the Elm St. or RD 1 slot is filled, the letters are sorted again by house or box number. Similarly, once cars for the local are all on one track, it is again sorted to put the cars in station order to save the local's crew a lot of

switching out on the busy main line.

You don't need a separate track for every possible place a freight car could go. In fact, you can switch cars into any sequence on two tracks. But it's better to have a track for each train that will be built at the same time, plus an arrival/departure track or two for trains that arrive in the meantime. The Allegheny Midland had only a handful of yard tracks in its main classification yard at Sunrise, Va. (fig. 4-8), but that was enough to build the next several departing trains. Once those trains were out of town, the same tracks could be reused to build other trains.

A careful look at departure times will provide strong clues as to the number of yard tracks that are needed. Or you can tailor the sched-

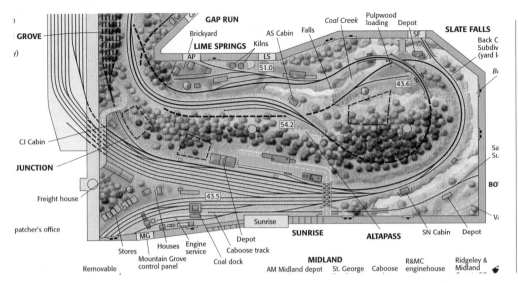

GROVE
CJ Cabin
JUNCTION
Freight house
patcher's office
Removable
Stores
Houses
Mountain Grove
control panel
MG
Engine
service
Coal dock
Depot
Caboose track
GAP RUN
Brickyard
LIME SPRINGS
AP
51.0
Kilns
LS
AS Cabin
Falls
Coal Creek
Pulpwood
loading
Depot
SF
SLATE FALLS
Back C
Subdiv
(yard l
43.6
54.2
43.5
Sunrise
SUNRISE
ALTAPASS
SN Cabin
Depot
MIDLAND
AM Midland depot   St. George   Caboose   R&MC
enginehouse
Ridgeley &
Midland
BO'
Sa
Su
Va

Fig. 4-8: This plan and two photos of the Allegheny Midland's yard main classification yard at Sunrise, Va., show it to be a compact facility. It was adequate to originate and terminate a north- and southbound local and two north- and two southbound freights. Several fast freights and all coal trains ran through on the main (limestone ballast). The view-blocking mountain to the left of the highway overpass was later removed to prevent a job action.

the widest part of a yard anyway. Rather, couple up to a cut of cars and drag it down to the lead where you can see what cars are on that track, then switch them accordingly. That is, bring the work to you, just as the pros do (fig. 4-9). And no car-forwarding system should require you to find cars randomly located in a yard. Keep track of what goes into and comes out of every track in real time (fig. 4-10).

You can reduce the work done in a yard by pre-sorting the blocks of inbound cars in staging. Another advantage is that model trains are typically much shorter than prototype trains. So where a prototype yard may require two eastbound and two westbound yard switchers, you may get by with only one or

two switchers, thanks to the shorter trains and the pre-blocked cars in staging.

For major yards, you may be able to have yard crews work from both sides of the yard by locating a yard-master's pit along the side away from the main aisle (fig. 4-11). This reduces the reach-in distance from both aisles and keeps some yard personnel out of main people-traffic areas.

Yards are not intended to be storage areas for trains or cars, although some tracks may indeed serve that function. Empty hoppers or grain boxcars, for example, may be stored in a yard as the busy shipping season approaches. But cars that stand still aren't earning money for anyone. If they're foreign cars, the railroad holding them at mid-

ule of trains to the available number of yard tracks. But how can we possibly hope to model a major classification yard, especially in HO or a larger scale? Even if we had

space for all those tracks, we couldn't reach in from the aisle to work them.

It's not as glum as it seems. For one thing, you shouldn't be reaching across night pays a small per diem fee, but that can add up.

Not all yards could be expanded as train lengths grew, so trains had to be "doubled" or even "tripled" out of the yard by yard or departing road crews as they joined cuts on two or three yards tracks. Some yards were equipped with "yard air" lines so that the air reservoirs on a soon-to-depart train could be filled, saving the time it would take for the road engine to pump up the train line.

Car inspectors, often called "car knockers" because of they way they banged on parts to test their integrity and slammed journal-box lids closed, inspected all cars. Their work contributed to safety, but it was obviously in their best interest to find cars that needed repair. Few trains arrived and departed without at least one car being marked for repair. Such cars had to be cut out of the train and switched to a repair-in-place, or RIP, track, a busy operation few choose to model. RIP-bound car could be selected by a roll of the dice, a "seven" designating the seventh car.

Similarly, cars often had to be cleaned before reuse, so there was typically a clean-out track in a remote corner of the yard, another operational feature that is too seldom modeled. All cars from,

Fig. 4-9: That railroader standing by the kaolin-filled boxcar isn't about to walk around the yard to see what's on each track. If need be, he'll have the yard engineer pull each track and make notes as the cars roll by.

Fig. 4-10: It's easy to keep track of what's on each track by putting each car card and waybill in a bill box labeled for that track at the same time the associated car is shoved into that track. Knowing the name of each track also helps to keep everything sorted out. Yard tracks are numbered going away from the main.

or for, a certain type of industry could be routed to the clean-out track.

Just as Andy's Ozark Lines plan provides, be sure the yard engine has a place to work off the main line (fig. 4-12). A yard lead or drill track is ideally as long as the longest yard track so that cars on any track can be pulled as a unit. Arrival and departure tracks should be located so that those moving trains don't get between the yard lead and the yard itself.

Passenger terminals

One of the most striking sights in railroading was a fast-approaching set of red-nosed Santa Fe F units on

Fig. 4-11 (below): Yards are like kitchens during a family reunion: They attract a crowd. To move the yardmaster out of the main aisle, designer Frank Hodina located Charleston yard on the author's NKP layout away from the perimeter wall.

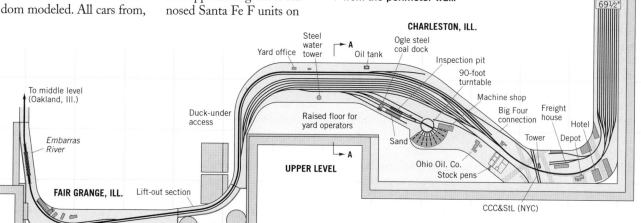

CHARLESTON, ILL.

Fourth Subdivision staging (to St. Louis)

69½"

To middle level (Oakland, Ill.)

Embarras River

FAIR GRANGE, ILL.   Lift-out section

Duck-under access

Raised floor for yard operators

UPPER LEVEL

Steel water tower
Yard office
Oil tank
Ogle steel coal dock
Inspection pit
90-foot turntable
Machine shop
Big Four connection
Freight house
Hotel
Depot
Tower
Sand
Ohio Oil. Co.
Stock pens
CCC&StL (NYC)

A

A

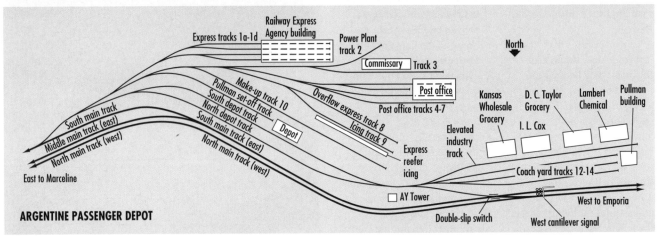

Express tracks 1a-1d
Railway Express
Agency building
Power Plant
track 2
Commissary Track 3
Make-up track 10
Pullman set-off track
South depot track
North depot track
South depot track
North main track (west)
South main track (east)
Middle main track (east)
North main track (west)
South main track
Overflow express track 8
Post office
Post office tracks 4-7
Icing track 9
Depot
Express reefer icing
Elevated industry track
North
Kansas Wholesale Grocery
D. C. Taylor Grocery
I. L. Cox
Lambert Chemical
Pullman building
Coach yard tracks 12-14
East to Marceline
AY Tower
Double-slip switch
West cantilever signal
West to Emporia

ARGENTINE PASSENGER DEPOT

Fig. 4-12 (top left): The NKP Alco RS-3 (top left) is switching the east end of the west-bound yard on the lead north of the main line in Frankfort, Ind. The eastbound yard is in the distance behind the coal dock in this view looking west from the Monon crossing tender's elevated shanty.

Fig. 4-13 (top right): Santa Fe's red war-bonnet scheme on a set of F units is an icon for the American passenger train. Here no. 212, the *Tulsan*, eases to a stop at Argentine, Kan., on Chuck Hitchcock's former HO railroad. The train will terminate here, but the rear two cars will continue to Chicago on no. 12. Chuck Hitchcock photo

the point of a stainless-steel passenger train (fig. 4-13). There was no doubt whatsoever that such trains were due the respect and admiration of everyone from operating crews to passengers. And the Santa Fe wasn't alone in operating a grand fleet of passenger trains.

To many modelers, the passenger train plays the role of an attractive nuisance: It looks cool but does little more than cause freights to clear its path at the appointed hour. Chuck Hitchcock, among others, looked more deeply into the operating potential of the passenger train, and his HO layout included an elaborate passenger facility at Argentine, Kan., that supported a lot of switching (fig. 4-14).

Each day, his Argentine Division of the Santa Fe operated a dozen passenger

trains, as he described in the 1997 edition of *Model Railroad Planning*. Switch lists (fig. 4-15) guided crews as they switched passenger trains on tight schedules. A chair car and a parlor-observation from no. 11, the *Kansas Cityan,* for example, were added to the consist of no. 211, the *Tulsan,* at Argentine. Storage-mail and working RPO cars were added to no. 19, the *Chief,* and a storage-mail car was removed for spotting at the post office.

The trains were parked in hidden staging tracks before and after use (fig. 4-16). Because of Chuck's considerable knowledge of ATSF passenger operations in the early 1950s, reusing the same consist during an operating session was not practical; each train had to be reblocked to reflect the flipside's different consist.

Fig. 4-14 (above): Argentine passenger station on Chuck Hitchcock's Santa Fe layout was compact yet offered a full range of head-end as well as coach and sleeper set-off and servicing tracks.

Turning trains for reuse as a different train during a session was therefore not warranted.

If you're modeling a rural stretch of main line, passenger trains may indeed be little more than short-lived operating hassles for freight and local crews to watch out for. But they add a sense of drama while keeping everyone on his or her toes and cognizant of the time. Local passenger trains that make frequent stops along the line add a little more interest to operations.

On mine branches into the coal fields, miners trains were run each morning and

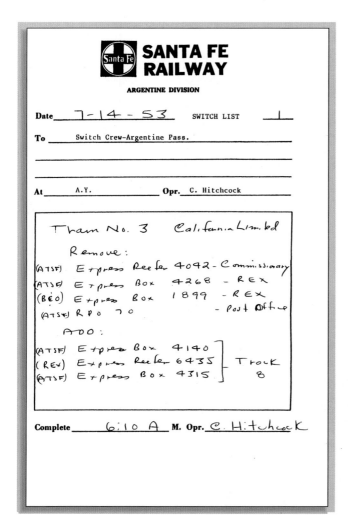

SANTA FE RAILWAY

ARGENTINE DIVISION

Date 7-14-53   SWITCH LIST   1

To   Switch Crew-Argentine Pass.

At   A.Y.   Opr. C. Hitchcock

Train No. 3   California Limited

Remove:

(ATSF) Express Reefer 4042 - Commissary
(ATSF) Express Box 4268 - REX
(B&O) Express Box 1899 - REX
(ATSF) RPO 70   - Post Office

ADD:

(ATSF) Express Box 4140 ⎤
(REX) Express Reefer 6435 ⎬ Track
(ATSF) Express Box 4315 ⎦   8

Complete   6:10 A M. Opr. C. Hitchcock

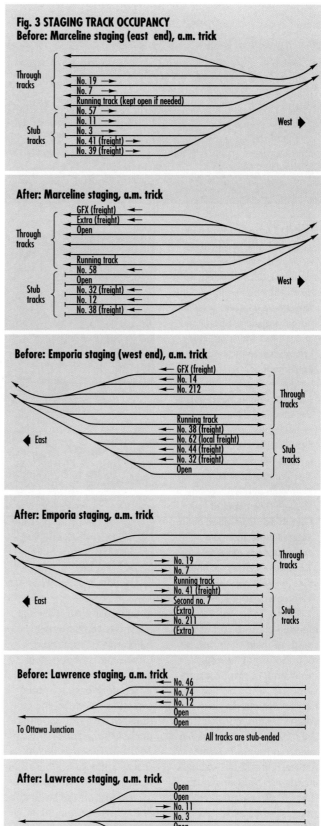

Fig. 3 STAGING TRACK OCCUPANCY
Before: Marceline staging (east end), a.m. trick

After: Marceline staging, a.m. trick

Before: Emporia staging (west end), a.m. trick

After: Emporia staging, a.m. trick

Before: Lawrence staging, a.m. trick

After: Lawrence staging, a.m. trick

Fig. 4-16 (above): These diagrams show the status of various Argentine Div. staging yards before and after each trick or operating segment. Open tracks provided flexibility for extras and specials.

evening. These ranged from the rattiest coaches the railroad owned (fig. 4-17) to gas-electrics trailing a coach (fig. 4-18) or even a string of hoppers trailed by a coach and/or combine. Budd Rail Diesel Cars (RDCs) provided some financial relief for railroads forced to continue passenger operations over main lines and branches that had few riders. Many of these conveyances were scheduled as first-class trains, and they therefore add operating interest to a model railroad.

Locomotive servicing

Engine servicing terminals (fig. 4-19) provide fuel and sand (for traction). Steam locos also require water, as do passenger diesels for train-heating boilers. The commonly heard expression

Fig. 4-15 (above): Hand-written switch lists were used to guide yard crews as they assembled passenger trains for departure on Hitchcock's Santa Fe Argentine Division. This list covers no. 3, the *California Limited.* Chuck's extensive research into ATSF passenger operations provided the background information needed to compile consist lists.

"Put the engine on the pit" comes from the need to spot a coal-fired steam engine over a water-filled pit where its firebox grates could be shaken to dump cinders. The cinders were hauled away in gons or hoppers, often for use as ballast.

The pit or "fueling pad" area is the usual place where road crews get on or off their road engine(s). Servicing

Fig. 4-17 (above left): An old wood combine (scratchbuilt by Jim Boyd) was deemed adequate to haul miners from their valley homes up into the hills where coal was wrested from the ground. Short lines and miners' trains offer an opportunity to model older equipment.

Fig. 4-18 (above right): A Brill gas-electric pulling an old coach hauled miners to work and brought mail and packages to remote mountain villages on the Coal Fork Extension of the Allegheny Midland. The depot at Low Gap, W. Va., was wiped out in a derailment, so an old caboose body got a new job. The train-order signal shows that the next northbound has 19 orders and/or a message.

inbound engines and, if necessary, moving them to the roundhouse for turning, inspection, or minor repairs is the job of the hostler. The hostler also checks the engine assignment board in the roundhouse and spots the needed outbound engines on the ready track. If a steam engine has been sitting on the ready track for some time, the road crew may top off the water before heading down into the yard to pick up their train.

An engine terminal can thus be a major "industry" on your model railroad. Inbound are hoppers filled with coal or tank cars filled with fuel oil, and covered hoppers filled with traction sand. Outbound are hoppers or gons filled with cinders.

You don't have to model everything in an engine terminal to have it function normally. On the Allegheny Midland, for example, the space-eating roundhouse and turntable were assumed to be located just off the layout (fig. 4-20). Steam engines couldn't be turned, but this was easily circumvented: One pair of steam-powered freights began the day as a northbound departure. The engine that came back southbound on the flip-side of that train later in the day didn't have to be turned until "tomorrow."

Another pair of freights had a southbound arrival at Sunrise before a northbound departure, but instead of turning the arriving engine, it just sat under the coal tipple. A second engine of the same class was on the pit ready to head north on the flip-side of that freight. The cost was an extra steam locomotive; the savings were a lot of space and complex construction. The space thus gained was used for much-needed arrival and departure tracks.

To learn more about engine-servicing facilities, I recommend *The Model*

Fig. 4-19 (above): The engine servicing facility at South Fork, W. Va., on the AM mainly tended to the Mallets that worked the mines up Cheat River Grade. It was small but had all of the basics: water, coal, sand, and pits to inspect the locomotives and dump the cinders. Diesel fueling cranes were added recently, a portent of things to come.

Railroader's Guide to Locomotive Servicing Terminals by Marty McGuirk (Kalmbach).

Staging yards

North American model railroads tend to have passive

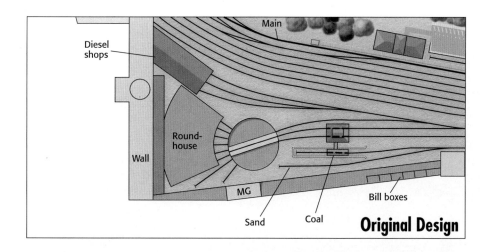

Original Design

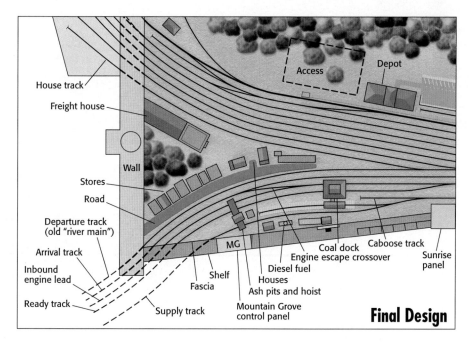

House track
Freight house
Wall
Stores
Road
Departure track
(old "river main")
Arrival track
Inbound
engine lead
Ready track
Supply track
Fascia
Shelf
MG
Houses
Diesel fuel
Ash pits and hoist
Mountain Grove
control panel
Engine escape crossover
Coal dock
Caboose track
Sunrise
panel
Access
Depot

Final Design

Fig. 4-20: These drawings show the Sunrise engine terminal as designed (left) and as later revised. The need to turn and house steam locomotives was less than the need for arrival, departure, and caboose tracks. These tracks simulated the old "river main," and the roundhouse was presumed to be located off to the left. The "new" main and yard were at the top—where they always were, but the new plan offered a different interpretation of the railroad's evolution. A freight house was needed when the AM was backdated to the steam era, so it was squeezed in at the left.

staging, as opposed to active fiddle, yards. These are often, but certainly not always, hidden from ready view so as to maintain the illusion that trains are coming from or going to distant places (fig. 4-21). They can be stub-ended (fig. 4-22) if trains are to be used but once per day (session), a space-saving design approach.

All trackwork in hidden yards must be absolutely top quality and as bulletproof as you can build it. Diode-matrix or DCC-decoder route-selection and track-occupancy detection are required to allow train crews to move largely unseen trains

in and out of the hidden yards reliably.

David Barrow's Cat Mountain & Santa Fe featured visible staging yards (fig. 4-23), which—unlike "muzzle-loading" stub-end staging yards—allowed the railroad to operate continuously. He modeled the 1970s, so seeing a number of trains with diesel locomotives sitting outside of town in a holding yard wasn't visually jarring. Doing that with steam power would have raised eyebrows.

Putting loop staging yards at both ends of the railroad allows trains to be reused during a session. This would

be a plus for railroads featuring heavy traffic such as a commuter line. Moreover, such trains tend to look alike, so the reuse of a given consist is unlikely to be noticed.

The down side is that loop staging yards take up a lot of floor space, and they have twice as much of everything from turnouts to switch motors, not to mention opportunities for problems—derailments at turnouts, failed switch mechanisms, and trains fouling ladders, to name a few.

Dan Zugelter faced an unusual need when he designed his Chesapeake & Ohio staging yard: The hid-

den yard represented the place where river-grade passenger locomotives were replaced with mountain engines. He also had to accommodate endless coal trains that always sent loaded hoppers headed east, empties west.

His solution was elegant: He connected both ends of the railroad at the staging yard so he could use, and reuse, the coal trains as needed after each train had paused a suitable interval in staging. That wouldn't work for the power-swapping passenger trains, however, so Dan added "fly-over" loops at both ends of the staging yard (fig. 4-24) so trains entering

Fig. 4-21 (above): We suspect that this Western Maryland freight rolling east around Helmstetter's Curve in May 1973 came from distant Connellsville, Pa.—but could it be coming out of a hidden staging yard just beyond those hills instead? Low hills, highway overpasses, tall buildings, even trees can be used to hide the entrances to staging yards.

Fig. 4-22 (right): Stub-ended staging yards conserve space and track components, but trains can be used only once per day. When all trains have been moved out of staging, the session is over. Shown here is the Allegheny Midland's north-end staging yard (which was later extended to avoid "doubling" long trains into two short tracks) near the end of an operating session. Between sessions, trains were backed out and reblocked, and loaded hoppers were shuttled back to tipples, empties to staging.

the yard with river-grade engines eastbound come back out of staging with the same engine westbound, and vice versa for westbound trains off the mountain. Each loop holds three passenger trains, which is sufficient for his schedule.

One argument in favor of loop staging yards is that trains can be pulled, rather than backed, out between sessions for reblocking consists. That argument is spurious, as reblocked trains still have to be backed into the staging tracks. Stub-ended

staging yards require trains to be backed out for reblocking, then backed into staging again, but this is not asking too much of well-built and -maintained trackwork and equipment.

Mike Hamer took a different approach to hidden stag-

Fig. 4-23: In more modern times, the sight of entire trains with locomotives sitting in an outlying yard is not unusual, so David Barrow was able to stage Cat Mountain & Santa Fe trains in a visible yard. Moreover, both ends of the main line connected to this yard, so trains could be reused with minor paperwork changes. Tommy Holt photo

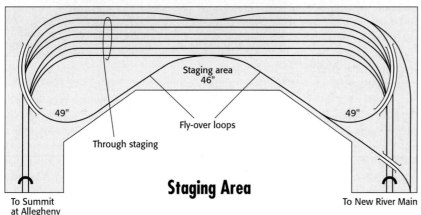

Staging Area

Fig. 4-24: Dan Zugelter's C&O staging yard allows passenger trains to be turned from either direction by negotiating fly-over loops, keeping powerful "mountain" engines in the hills and "flatlands" power on the river grades. Through staging tracks allow loaded eastbound coal trains and empty westbounds to continue in the desired directions without loading or unloading hoppers.

ing, as he explained in his article on "Surround staging" in the 2001 issue of *Model Railroad Planning:* He located the staging yards around the perimeter of the layout behind a low backdrop (fig. 4-25). Little room area was sacrificed, and he avoided having to deal with a staging yard just below the main benchwork or one reached by a helix.

Fiddle yards

Fiddle yards, or active staging yards, got their start in the United Kingdom. A lack of space for large home layouts led to the modeling of single town scenes, often

spectacularly well done. Trains came into town out of a hidden yard, did their thing, and either continued on to another hidden yard or, more typically, returned to the original yard.

If the hidden yard was a passive staging yard, at most a half dozen or so trains could be operated, which was insufficient during busy public exhibitions. The Brits therefore quickly devised a number of schemes that allowed them to "fiddle with" cars and locomotives: take them off the hidden yard tracks and replace them with new consists. Several experienced U.S. operators such as Lee

Nicholas (fig. 4-26) and Jack Ozanich have adopted fiddle yards to allow continuous operation. Someone acts as a "mole" yardmaster in the hidden fiddle yard, breaking down arriving trains and building new ones, for as long as the crews want to operate.

Determining staging needs

How many staging tracks do you need? It depends on two factors: how many trains you run and their schedule. If you expect to run six eastbounds and six westbounds, you'll need more than six staging tracks unless you coordinate arrivals and departures with computer-

like precision. I tried to leave four to six hours "fast-time" between the time a train departed from a staging track until another train heading into staging was scheduled to take its place.

Paul Faulk automated the tricky scheduling task by using personal-computer spreadsheet software, as he described in *Model Railroad Planning* 1997. In a nutshell, he made a table listing the time that each train arrives at or departs from a staging yard track. He then used the equation $S = T + (A - D)$, where S is the number of staging tracks in use at any given time, T is the total

Fig. 4-25 (above left): Mike Hamer located staging for his HO Boston & Maine RR around the perimeter of the layout behind a low backdrop, which assured easy overhead access, as he explained in *Model Railroad Planning* 2001. Peter Nesbitt photo

Fig. 4-26 (above right): Lee Nicholas plays the role of the "mole" on his Utah Colorado Western. This hidden fiddle (active staging) yard is worked during an operating session to make up new trains in "real time," allowing operating sessions to continue in "op till you drop" fashion. Lou Sassi photo

number of trains to run, A is an arrival event, and D is a departure event. He translated that formula into terms the spreadsheet software understood to get a figure for the total number of staging tracks needed. "Don't forget that you may want to run an extra train," he cautioned. And you'll need to pad the figures to allow for late-running trains.

No matter how sharp your pencil, however, odds are that you'll underestimate the number of staging tracks. Based on experience with the Allegheny Midland, the correct answer can be calculated using a simple formula: N = 2n + 1, where "n" is the number of staging tracks you *think* you need, and "N" is the number you *actually* need. I did more homework before designing staging for my new layout, however, so I hope I won't have to later extend and retrofit more staging tracks, as I did on the AM.

Veteran track planner Don Mitchell and others have recommended sequential staging, where more than one train is staged on a track.

Since you know in advance the order in which those trains will be used, this approach can be helpful if you have more length than width for a staging yard.

Running trains back into hidden staging in a sequential manner is more problematic, as you don't want the subsequent trains plowing into the first ones that entered each staging track. There are a number of detection devices on the market that allow operators to know with precision where their trains are located, and this process can even be automated.

On-line staging

There are other places where staging can be used to advantage. On the Allegheny Midland, for example, I extended the Sunrise yard lead to the edge of the benchwork to make it appear to be a truncated branch. Between sessions, a branch local (fig. 4-27) was staged on the lead/branch; as soon as the clock started, this local was run on into the yard, which (1) provided more inbound traffic variety,

(2) freed up the yard lead for switching, and (3) returned a locomotive for other use.

A Baltimore & Ohio local was similarly staged on line at South Fork, W. Va. It immediately "continued" its run into town as the session began, leaving its cars on the AM interchange track. This opened up one leg of a wye track behind the enginehouse. The B&O crew tied up and slept at the local railroad YMCA hotel during the day, then gathered up cars delivered by the AM and went back home very well rested that night.

Fig. 4-28 shows all of the staging that fed the visible (scenicked) areas of the AM. This included a Western Maryland local that worked the AM interchange at North Durbin, W.Va., then continued into staging. For that train to return later, a second engine with the same number was required, as there wasn't room for a return loop.

Fig. 4-27 (above): The Sunrise yard lead was extended around the bend past SN Cabin, then truncated at the edge of the benchwork to simulate a branch line. A branch local was visibly staged on this track; as the session began, it immediately came into the yard, freeing up the lead and releasing the locomotive for yard or other duties.

Stub-ended mine branches were handled either by operating them as a turn out of South Fork during the day or by staging them up on the branch. In the latter case, they came down the branch as the day began, laid over in South Fork, and headed back up the branch into staging at the end of the day. Again, this circumvented the need for a space-eating loop at the end of the branch.

Restaging the railroad

One of the major advantages of a loop-type staging

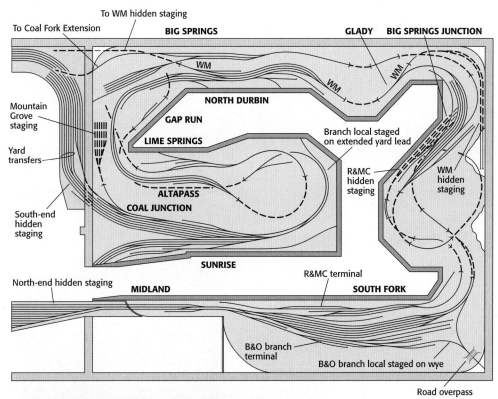

To Coal Fork Extension
To WM hidden staging
BIG SPRINGS
GLADY **BIG SPRINGS JUNCTION**
WM
WM
WM
WM
NORTH DURBIN
GAP RUN
LIME SPRINGS
Branch local staged on extended yard lead
Mountain Grove staging
Yard transfers
R&MC hidden staging
WM hidden staging
ALTAPASS
COAL JUNCTION
South-end hidden staging
SUNRISE
R&MC terminal
North-end hidden staging
MIDLAND
SOUTH FORK
B&O branch terminal
B&O branch local staged on wye
Road overpass

Fig. 4-28: The hidden and visible staging that fed the Allegheny Midland, Western Maryland, and Ridgeley & Midland County on the author's HO layout is shown here. There were 6 south-end staging tracks for the V&O, and 6 more were added for the joint AM-V&O coal yard at Mountain Grove. The north-end staging yard was expanded from 6 to 13 tracks. A pair of staging tracks served each end of the WM, and the R&MC staging comprised 5 tracks.

Fig. 4-29 (left): All of the work done by mine shifters (here at Low Gap) and coal drags has to be undone between sessions by moving loaded hoppers (or hopper loads) back to tipples and empties into staging yards. This gives the layout owner, who typically dispatches or acts as a supervisor during operating sessions, a chance to test-run the entire railroad.

yard is that you can get your trains back for reuse, either during the session or between sessions. This is of special value if you operate a lot of look-alike, single-block trains such as commuter trains, unit coal trains, reefer blocks, and so forth.

The advantages disappear with open loads such as coal hoppers or when loose-car freights are the norm. In the latter instance, cars blocked correctly for an eastbound move may be wildly out of order after the waybills are cycled for the flip-side westbound move of that consist. Some software programs

accommodate such needs, but in any event it isn't a show stopper. Simply run such trains back out of staging, cycle the waybills, and use a switch engine or the good ol' 0-5-0 (your hand) to reblock the cars to put them in proper order for a westbound move. Then back the train into staging.

If you have coal mines or other operations such as rock crushers and gravel pits, you face a different problem: Loads picked up at a tipple either have to be removed from the cars and dropped into empties at the tipple, or the loaded cars have to be

moved back under the tipples between sessions (fig. 4-29).

I found trying to remove and keep track of various types (nut, pea, egg, stoker, lump, etc) of coal loads was a substantial pain, usually derailing cars, so I simply ran the loads back to the tipples, picked up the empties there, and ran the empties back to a staging yard. This gave me a chance to operate the railroad on my own, which was not only fun but helpful in that I usually discovered several operational glitches such as low couplers or dirty wheels.

Passenger trains also had to be switched end for end or

run back to the other end of the railroad; I chose to do the latter rather than switch or manhandle the cars. Since most large-layout owners act as dispatcher or host and trouble-shooter during operating sessions (or, thinking more positively, like the conductor of an orchestra), taking advantage of a chance to run one's railroad while restaging it sounds like a good idea anyway.

CHAPTER FIVE

Shortcuts to operation

Fig. 5-1: Quick, now—can you tell which units had the plastic grab irons replaced with wire ones? The author installed wire grabs on Allegheny Midland diesels (above left), but Allen McClelland got visually equal results on most V&O units by focusing on more obvious details and a great weathering job (above right). W. Allen McClelland photos

Few of us have as much time to spend on our model railroads as we'd like. We therefore need to make every hour count. We can do that by using the available time efficiently, and by adjusting our priorities to make more time available for the railroad.

Regular operating sessions are a great way to "create" time for the hobby. You reserve an afternoon or evening for each session once a week or month. You also find time to stage the railroad prior to the next session. And you allocate time for any maintenance items or upgrades, including finishing new projects that you're eager to show the gang. If it weren't for the upcoming session, you might spend that time on other less noble pursuits.

Fig. 5-2: You can yell all you want, but crew members will pick up or push equipment on occasion, such as a balky coupling maneuver. Although most operators are sensitive to ever-increasing quality standards, details added to models intended for frequent operation should be sturdy enough to withstand such handling.

Fig. 5-3: Mike DelVecchio did a great job assembling this resin kit, and the realistic details were soon augmented with realistic damage when the car was sideswiped by a local crew. Repairs might accent the damage with rusty scrape marks rather than restoring the model. In either event, a trip to the RIP track is warranted.

Moreover, one operating railroad tends to beget another. Soon there are several operating layouts in the area for you and your friends to enjoy. When your enthusiasm ebbs, as it eventually will, someone else will be excited about some aspect of the hobby, and his or her enthusiasm tends to rub off. Even gentle hints—"Operating this month?"—have a way of nudging you back into a model railroading frame of mind.

Operation brings focus to the hobby. Your choice of modeling projects will begin to revolve around what you need to make operating sessions more interesting and realistic. You won't buy just any car or structure kit but instead will select those that complement your railroad in the chosen era and locale. You'll also buy books and videotapes that provide information about the railroads in that region and era so as to gain a better understanding about what your railroad should look like and how it should operate.

What's "good enough"?

When the primary purpose of a model railroad becomes realistic operation, everything else assumes a supporting role. Models no longer have to stand on their own merits, as they are merely one part of a large cast of characters. You can still build a depot to best-in-show standards, but in an operating context it won't do a better job than a carefully painted and weathered plastic kit.

Where do we draw the line? Surely every structure and car can't be built to prize-winning standards or we'll never get the railroad built. Allen McClelland uses the term "good enough" to describe a necessary and sufficient quality of modeling for the operating railroad. Although his Virginian & Ohio boasts some blue-ribbon-winning models, most are basic kits, typically kitbashed better to fill a specific need. Look at them carefully and you'll find they aren't intended to be contest winners. Look at them in the context of the entire railroad, however, and they are more than good enough to do the job. They look right.

Consider the grab irons on his diesel fleet. While I usually replace the plastic grab irons molded onto shells with wire grabs (fig. 5-1),

Allen simply highlights the plastic ridges with paint or ignores them completely. Not once during many operating sessions on the V&O have I, or anyone else within earshot, noticed the lack of individual grab irons on V&O units—or the presence thereof on Allegheny Midland units. Obviously, the molded-on grabs are good enough in the context of the V&O as an operating railroad. The extra work lavished on AM units may make me feel more comfortable, which is nice, but it's not productive.

Many modelers take considerable pride in the quality of their models, especially where rolling stock is concerned. The plethora of resin freight car kits attests to this. Fortunately, one-piece bodies have made assembling such kits much easier, which saves time, which affords more time for building and operating the railroad.

Do such finely detailed models stand up to the rigors of operation? This is a touchy subject, as they are much more prone to damage when a car is re-railed or even uncoupled (fig. 5-2). Many modelers cut the "air hoses" off magnetically actuated

couplers to improve their appearance, but this requires inserting some sort of blade or pointed stick between the couplers' knuckles to spring them apart, and delicate details can be damaged in the process.

The bottom line is that the principles of good enough also apply to building models that won't cause you to suffer a panic attack every time a visitor goes near one, yet meet your quality standards for detail accuracy and completeness. There's no reason why a finescale model railroad built to exacting standards can't be operated flawlessly, but the potential for damage is there (fig. 5-3). If that leads to hard feelings or worry among crew members, perhaps the quest for detail has overridden the greater joys of enjoying the hobby with knowledgeable and dedicated modeling friends who are nevertheless human.

Place holders

Crews need to understand at a glance what's expected of them. If they arrive in a town with nary a clue as to what goes where, and why, they will be confused and intimidated. A barren siding that the layout owner knows will

Fig. 5-4 (left): No time to scratchbuild or kitbash a coal tipple? Rather than leaving the purpose of the siding to the mine shifter crew's imagination, placing a coal conveyor and/or front-end loader there makes the point. (Also see fig. 5-6.)

Fig. 5-5: Coal truck dumping ramps are usually simple affairs like this one along the Clinchfield (top). The author kitbashed one based on an East Broad Top design (above) from an Accurail plastic overpass kit, Central Valley steps, and a styrene chute.

one day serve a lumberyard does nothing to help crews get the work done.

Fortunately, there are several easy ways to help crews without compromising the finished product—a scratch-built model, perhaps, that will one day take its place on this siding. You can put a folded 3 x 5 card alongside the spur with the lumber-yard's name printed on it. You could even place several such cards to tell crews that boxcars filled with lumber go here while hoppers filled with coal go over there. Better yet, put a coal conveyor where the hopper should be

spotted (fig. 5-4) or a simple truck dump (fig. 5-5).

If you're willing to spend a few bucks, assemble an inexpensive plastic kit and drop it alongside the siding for now. A couple of those kits might be kitbashed into something more closely resembling the prototype (fig. 5-6). Or you can make a photocopy of a plan or side-view photograph of the lumberyard and dry-mount it to a piece of card-stock, then prop it up alongside the siding.

A caveat: Kitbashed models can turn out so well that you're never motivated to go back and replace them with

the intended craftsman kit or scratchbuilt model. On a freelanced railroad, this is usually of no great consequence, but a prototype-based railroad can start to edge away from its basis in reality if too many for-now structures are plopped down and never replaced. Nevertheless, the short-term need is to offer visual clues as to where to spot cars.

Signature structures

"Signature" structures are those that make it easy to understand the purpose of a piece of railroad. In Appalachia, it could be a

small coal tipple or a major coal preparation plant (fig. 5-7) or a pulpwood log or wood-chip loading facility (fig. 5-8). Paper making is also common to the South, New England, Midwest, and Pacific Northwest, plus much of Canada (fig. 5-9). In the prairie states, grain elevators punctuate the vastness like huge exclamation points (fig. 5-10). Along western narrow-gauge lines, mines and ore stamping mills were ubiquitous (fig. 5-11).

Such structures make communicating operational goals much easier. At a glance, even a first-time visi-

Fig. 5-6: The author never got around to scratchbuilding the Dixie Coal Co. tipple at Pikesville, Ky. (right), so he kitbashed a stand-in (below, background) in one evening from a Con-Cor "Tucson Silver Mine" kit, an Atlas watchman's shanty, and a Life-Like shed. The tipple in the foreground is also a stand-in for an Atomic Fuel Co. tipple at Berta (Haysi), Va., on the Clinchfield. It was quickly kitbashed using left-over Walthers coal mine parts and part of a City Classic's factory.

tor can grasp what the railroad's all about. That leaves only the details of how to do it for you to communicate.

It's therefore worth while to consider scratchbuilding or carefully kitbashing such structures, or at least ensuring that kit-built structures do the job from both a visual and an operating standpoint. You can afford to fudge a bit on a background structure, but that big mill around which the operation of the railroad hinges is worth doing well. Besides, this *is* a model-building hobby; enjoyable as running trains realistically can be, don't overlook the rewards of model building.

Layout size

How much railroad do you actually need to support realistic operation? Frankly, you can feed a one-town railroad from a staging or fiddle yard and keep yourself and maybe a friend or two busy for several hours at a time. Building a big layout that promises to fulfill your every dream may instead bog you down with the enormity of the task ahead. It's better to start small and then expand as goals and desires evolve and space allows.

Fig. 5-7: "Signature" structures, which set the tone for the entire railroad, are important enough to spend some time on. The coal prep plant and deep mine at Summerlee (above) on the Virginian near Oak Hill, W. Va., brought coal to the surface using the elevator tower at right. Coal from a nearby mine on the C&O was also brought in by hopper, dumped, and cleaned, so it was a loads in/loads-out facility to some extent. "Bony" (shale) was dumped into trucks at right, then successively larger sizes of screened coal from almost dust to pea, nut, egg, stoker, lump, etc., were routed to a specific track. The author built a representative model (top right) from several Walthers mines plus a scratchbuilt hoist tower.

That's why I advocate starting with one or more Layout Design Elements such as Wingate, Ind., which was described in chapter 2. You can always expand by building more LDEs, and you'll know from the get-go that what you're building is well rooted in prototype practice, even if you understand it imperfectly now. If you have a lot of space but limited time, build one or more LDEs and then add more LDEs as time allows. If you plan to

go for the gold right now, it's still a matter of stringing together a number of LDEs until you have depicted the key parts of the railroad(s) you're modeling or using as a benchmark for freelancing.

Modelers can be as greedy as heads of state when it comes to land acquisition, but be careful what you wish for. You can spend so much time planning and building a large model railroad that you never get around to getting it running, at least as well as it should. Don't compromise construction standards to save time and/or money.

It's not clear that having less space for a layout actually

saves time. Smaller layouts tend to be more intensively detailed than larger ones (fig. 5-12). You probably have a rather clear idea of how much railroad you want, how much space you have available, and what resources you can bring to bear to achieve that goal. If you really want something, there's a way to get there from here.

A well-built model railroad need not be a maintenance headache. My former 24 x 29-foot Allegheny Midland (plus a later 13 x 19-foot branch) required very little between-session maintenance. Yet some small railroads are maintenance night-

Fig. 5-8 (above): A small mill on the Western Maryland at Laurel Bank (Slatyfork), W. Va., converted logs into wood chips, which were transported to the Westvaco paper mill at Luke, Md., in extended-side former coal hoppers. Walthers makes a similar chip hopper kit.

mares. What's the difference?

The AM was built on a solid 1 x 4 framework. The subroadbed was $3/4''$ plywood. Tortoise and Hankscraft slow-motion switch motors were used instead of noisy and often maintenance-intensive solenoid switch machines. The Dynatrol

command-control system's constant voltage on the track ensured a continuous current flow from rail through wheel to receiver (decoder) and, when desired, motor. Command control also precluded a huge number of wires between blocks and rotary switches, each soldered and screwed connection and switch contact being a maintenance liability.

A separate room with a wallboard ceiling and carpeted floor kept dust to a minimum, so much so that track usually had to be

cleaned only after a major construction project. And I personally handlaid all visible track, which meant extra care was lavished on every inch of it. That ensured against kinks, sharp vertical curves, and other glitches that trip up smooth operation.

The railroad operated formally only once each month. Between sessions, however, trains moved back to their staged positions—notably loaded hoppers back to tipples and empty hoppers back to staging tracks or yards. This took me only a few

Fig. 5-9 (top): This modern sawmill and wood-chip plant was scratchbuilt by Patrick Lawson for his HO Cascade Div. of CP Rail. It's based on a prototype at Maple Ridge, B.C. The green steel structure is the wood chip loader. Patrick Lawson photo

hours. A train or two also moved when visitors stopped by. Despite this relatively modest amount of activity, when it was time to operate, the railroad responded.

The bottom line: One person can build and maintain a

Fig. 5-10 (above): Grain elevators, aptly described as the sentinels of the prairies, are signature structures for granger railroads. In the steam era, grain was shipped in clean, tight 40-foot boxcars, but 100-ton covered hoppers took over in the diesel era. They don't consume much layout space; Bernie Kempinski built this N scale scene on a narrow shelf (see *Model Railroad Planning* 2001). Bernie Kempinski photo

large home layout if it is built right from the get-go in a prepared space.

Odds and ends

It's usually not productive to build a model railroad through the scenery stage before operating it (fig. 5-13). There's nothing like an operating session to point out flaws in the logic used to design a railroad. A missing crossover that makes a runaround move difficult will become quite obvious during the first few sessions.

Moreover, regular operating sessions mean regular visits by crew members, which will motivate progress. You may come to trust some of them to help you with construction. Even if you then help them with their own layouts, thus slowing progress on yours, the pooling of talent, ideas, tools, and experience will more than offset this temporary loss. Much construction time is actually spent rebuilding something,

Fig. 5-13 (right): Veteran operators know that the secret to making progress on all aspects of a layout is to get it running as soon as possible. This uncovers trackwork and electrical bugs and maintains enthusiasm as one plods through the more mundane aspects of layout construction. In this 1995 photo, Perry Squier switches loaded hoppers at St. Marys, Pa., on his ca.-1923 Pittsburg, Shawmut & Northern. Most of the scenery has since been completed.

and working with experienced friends minimizes such wastage. Besides, it's usually less enjoyable to work alone.

You mind find, however, that having helpers shifts your role to that of a general contractor rather than a builder. You have to plan enough jobs before the gang arrives to keep everyone busy, or a general bull session will shortly and surely ensue. If that's not your style—you may get enough people-management challenges at work every day—then politely decline offers of assistance.

Getting at least some part of the railroad running right away is a good objective. It's a nice change of pace to run something, and you can start regular, semi-formal operating sessions that much sooner. You may want to build a portable staging yard (fig. 5-14) to give your trains a place to come from and go to, moving it east or west as the railroad is completed.

Don't be too proud to run out-of-the-box cars and locomotives in an effort to get the railroad to an operational point. Friends who are much farther along with their layouts may have had time to replace some lower-

Fig. 5-14 (right): The U.S.S. *Vancouver,* otherwise known as "the battleship," serves as a temporary staging yard on Bob Willer's HO Spokane, Portland & Seattle. The movable staging yard is shifted to accommodate new construction on the main line. A similar yard, perhaps on adjustable casters, could also support one or both ends of a one-town layout. Chuck Hitchcock photo

quality rolling stock with resin-kit models, for example, and they'll be happy to sell you their displaced fleet, perhaps with Kadee couplers still attached, for a modest sum. If and when you finally have time to complete enough high-quality cars to replace those stand-ins, sell them to the next guy to help him or her hold regular operating sessions.

Modeling a specific prototype can also be a time-saver, as it's easy for friends to understand your objectives without endlessly interrogating you about them. I have had total strangers walk up to me at National Model Railroad Association conventions to offer a photo or document that turned out to be very helpful. Once your modeling goals are clear, oth-

ers who share his interests or happen to have related information can and will come forward to help. Their legwork will save you time.

Just remember that you shouldn't become a sump for information. Repay those

who help you by sharing what you have found elsewhere. Invite them over to see the railroad that was made better, thanks to their help.

CHAPTER SIX

Forwarding cars

Fig. 6-1: Here's how all that lumber was unloaded at local lumber yards or team tracks: a board at a time! Loading the car was equally tedious. In December 1973, a crew unloads a carload of Canadian lumber on the original Norfolk Southern. Today, lumber is usually shipped in bundles on center-beam flatcars.

Moving cars to customers is what freight railroading is all about (fig. 6-1).

Before trains can move, however, they have to be assembled a car or a cut at a time (fig. 6-2). Model railroaders have devised a number of clever ways to forward cars to destinations. I'll briefly review several of them, then cover one of the most common and popular methods, car cards and waybills (sometimes called the "card order" system), in considerable detail.

Form 280 **MIDLAND ROAD** 5-63
SWITCH AND INTERCHANGE CARD

TRAIN NO. _____ FROM Sunrise TO _____
CONDUCTOR _____ ENG. NO. _____
DEPT. _____ M. DATE _____
ARRIVED _____ M. DATE _____
BILLS CALLED FOR _____ M. RECD _____

KIND CAR	INITIAL	NO.	CONTENTS	FROM/TRKS	TO. ETC.
H	NKP	66725	nut coal	3	Clint Elec
	AM	30765			
	AM	30921			
↓	V&O	4432			
X	NKP	4076	boxes	2	Amer Std
T	GATX	91484	gasoline	↓	Mid Oil
↓	↓	99743	↓	3	McNamara Pa.
R	PFE	17348	MTY	)	Chicago
↓	↓	17851		)	
X	AM	4532	LCL	1	SR
G	AM	61071	MTY	2	BJ
↓	↓	61101			
X	C&NW	83142		3	Chicago
	UP	77104			
↓	ATSF	554321			
↓	MS+L	7024	↓	↓	↓
L	AM	99443	sand	1	SR
H		32707	stkr coal	)	SR
		32501		)	
		36622		)	
X	V&O	4079	paint	3	Canton O.
↓	VM	33245	↓	↓	↓
LP	V&O	49121	pulpwood	2	ND
↓	↓	49137	↓	↓	↓

Fig. 6-2 (far left): Just as lumber is unloaded a stick, or a few sticks, at a time, cars or short cuts of cars are switched into trains. Locating the main line along one side of the yard and providing a separate switching lead allows yard crews to do their work with a minimum of interruptions, as at Sunrise, Va., on the Allegheny Midland.

Fig. 6-3 (left): Professional railroaders use a switch list form to list the cars in a cut they need to switch. Each car's reporting marks and road number are listed along with its contents and destination. The yardmaster or foreman then decides which cars go into which yards tracks and marks that on the right side of the list. Such lists are often made up and used by local crews out on the road.

Switch lists

Professional railroaders usually switch cuts of cars by referring to a switch list (fig. 6-3). This is a standard form on which cars in an inbound train or a yard track are listed. The yardmaster then marks which track each car goes on so as to sort them into destination-based blocks for forwarding in trains.

In this example, the Allegheny Midland yardmaster at Sunrise, Va., has designated yard track 1 for cars that are to be delivered in town ("propers"), track 2 for cars billed to this division ("shorts"), and track 3 for cars for the next division-point yard or beyond it ("throughs"). The term "proper" also refers to a car destined for delivery at the next division point.

The yardmaster then uses his or her knowledge of local industries and towns on the adjoining division to write down a "1" or a "2" beside those car on the list that should be sorted into tracks 1 and 2. Cars for myriad destinations beyond those towns are marked for track 3.

The cars for the northbound local on track 2 would then be resorted to put them in station order to ease the local's job. The local's crew thus won't have to waste time out on the road switching cars. To block cars in station order requires that the yard crew knows the order of the towns along that division, which they do from sheer repetition.

Some railroads made this job even easier by specifying the milepost of each station on the switch list. It's easy to put a car for station 54 behind a car for 25 and ahead of a car for 78. To the delight of their crews, some layout owners have emulated this practice.

Allen McClelland named stations in alphabetical order as an aid to crews. A car for Fullerton would therefore be blocked behind a car for Clintwood but ahead of a car for Indian Hill.

Cars for the next division point and beyond on track 3 might also be resorted into blocks to ease the work load at the next yard and thus expedite the passage of a fast freight. Switching cuts of cars in blocks and blocks into trains is a simple, iterative process. Don't get overwhelmed by the sight of a yard filled with freight cars going who knows where.

The waybills "know" where each car is going, so all you have to do is to pull one track at a time, sort the cars into yard tracks by destination, and then arrange those blocks into trains (fig. 6-4). If you encounter a few cars that will go into trains you're not now switching, stick them aside on a "for now" track and worry about them later. Making a switch list may take a little time up front yet save time overall by cutting down on mis-moves once the action starts.

The potential problem with switch lists on a model railroad is that you either have to take time to handwrite the lists before or during each operating session— a reasonable chore on a small layout but not on a large one—or a computer has to print them out. Computers assume all cars were moved correctly during the last session and haven't been touched since, so the lists they generate may be incorrect. Those who prepare the lists manually have to make-on-the-spot decisions as each car's contents (lading), if any, and where it is going. That takes time and considerable mental effort.

The good news for operators who use car cards and waybills is that crew members who like switch lists can simply take a few minutes before working the yard or switching the local to make up their own list based on data gleaned from the individual waybills.

Fig. 6-5 (left): Ed Ravenscroft and other pioneering operators used a color-coded tack system. It can be as simple as putting all green-tacked cars on the green-tacked yard track and sending them to Greentown, then spotting them according to a number on the tack. Linn Westcott photo

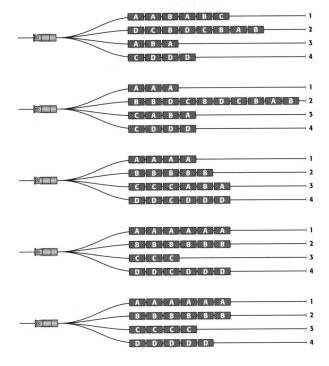

Fig. 6-4 (left): Once you get the hang of it, you can save a lot of needless moves by thinking ahead. The original yard arrangement is shown at top. Pull track 1, then put all A cars on 1, Bs on 2, etc. Then pull track 2 and so the same thing, then tracks 3 and 4. The train for destination A is now ready to go. "A" could be a town switched by the local or a distant city beyond the next classification yard.

Each arriving freight had a tack on each car, and the yardmaster sorted, say, the cars with blue tacks into a yard track marked with a blue tack just beyond the ladder turnout.

The Ridge Switch, a local on Ed's Glencoe Skokie Valley, comprised all blue-tack-coded cars. At each town, the local's crew found cars with tacks of various colors, and they picked up all cars except those with blue tacks. Set-outs were made according to each car's alpha code. Before leaving town, crews removed all tacks from the cars, signifying they had arrived at their destinations. Between sessions, Ed put new tacks on the cars to create new car movements. No effort was made to specify the lading in each car.

More information on Ed's

"waytack" system appeared on pages 78–81 of February 1979 *Railroad Model Craftsman* and pages 20–25 of July 1965 *Model Railroader*.

A similar system employs paper tabs, washers, or strips of Plastruct or Evergreen plastic I-beams (fig. 6-6). Andy Sperandeo documented this method on pages 84–88 of December 1981 *Model Railroader*, crediting John Allen as an early user of what he called the tab-on-car, or simply tab, system. Color codes are used, with one big color swatch and one smaller one on each side of the tab. Cars go to the location noted by the big color code, then to the small one; after the tab is turned over, the big-little process repeated.

One color goes farther than you might first imagine. Red, for example, could be all towns on one division served by one local. A dry-transfer letter or two can then designate individual towns and even spots within that town, as NP for North Durbin Pulpwood track. Andy's article covered the system's many permutations and opportunities in considerable detail.

Wheel reports matrix

MR senior editor Jim Hediger devised a simple car-forwarding system he

Colored tacks and tabs

One of the oldest systems for routing cars, made popular by pioneers such as John Allen, Roy Dohn, and Ed Ravenscroft, was the color-coded tack (or CCT) system (fig. 6-5). A new operator could walk right into one of Ed's session, for example, get a quick briefing on the color coding, and go right to work. The down side is that tacks on top of cars detract from their realism. On the other hand, crews grow accustomed to the tacks. You de-

cide whether you view each car primarily as a game piece or a realistic model; if the latter, a tack or other car-top system may not be for you.

Freight cars had holes drilled in the roof where a standard thumb tack could be inserted. Ed applied an 18-point black letter to the head of each tack to denote a specific spot within a color-coded area. The underside of each tack specified the type of car it was suitable for, which avoided routing a stock car into a lumber yard.

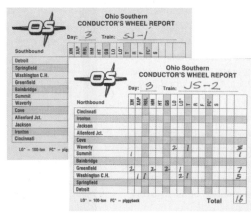

calls a wheel report (fig. 6-7). On a full-size railroad, the conductor made out a wheel report based on the waybills that specified which cars were in his train. Jim uses two forms on his Ohio Southern: yellow for northbound trains, green for southbound.

Stations' names in the order train crews will encounter them are printed along the left side of the card. Cars types (abbreviated) appear across the top. Jim fills in the date and train designation and specifies how many cars of each type go to each town based on industries there.

The train is switched in the yard based on the car types, which are arranged in blocks for each town. If the first town should receive two covered hoppers and one tank car, the tank car will be placed behind the covered hoppers (AAR designation "LO"—see the Appendix for other common car-type codes) for safety. When the crew gets to a town, it swaps inbound cars for a like number and type of outbound cars, so the number of cars in the consist remains constant. As with the waytack system, car lading is not specified. Open cars such as hoppers have removable coal loads,

which are swapped between sessions to ensure loaded cars are at the mines.

Jim has prepared 11 different sets of wheel reports. He uses set 4 if the operating session happens to occur on the 4th day of that month. For dates after the 11th, he adds the calendar date's digits; October 28th would use set 10 (2 + 8).

More information on Jim's wheel report system appeared in May 1984 MR.

Car cards and waybills

One of the most popular car-forwarding schemes is the card-order system using car cards and waybills, which was initially described in the December 1961 *Model Railroader* by the late Doug Smith. It seems to have more advocates than most, and the needed forms are available commercially.

I've used versions of this system for over a quarter of a century, and it has evolved as better ways of using it have surfaced or concerns have been addressed. At this writing, for example, I'm looking for ways to make the forms look more like actual waybills. Perhaps I'll abandon it entirely in the quest for greater realism.

The problem with wholesale change is that so many

experienced operators are familiar with the 4-cycle waybills produced by Old Line Graphics. A completely different system could create a steep learning curve and myriad mistakes during an operating session, especially with "visiting firemen." Only if I can find or create a system with vastly greater realism coupled to similar flexibility and ease of use will I embrace a major change. But it doesn't hurt to keep looking!

Understand up front that the car card and waybill system is not necessarily the best system. It does, however, have many attributes: It is surprisingly realistic, flexible, and versatile for such a simple system; it requires no special equipment such as computer software to set up or maintain (some regard this as a disadvantage!); it can be set up one car at a time; it is forgiving in that car-movement mistakes are easily detected and corrected; and it is so widely used that most operators understand it.

At this writing, the primary sources for car card and waybill forms are Old Line Graphics, Rail Group, and the NMRA's Operations SIG (see the Appendix for contact information). Quaker Valley Software markets a

Fig. 6-6 (above left): John Allen and others, including Kalmbach staff members who operated the Milwaukee, Racine & Troy, used easy to make and decipher color-coded tabs. Both sides of each tab have a large and a small color swatch; cars go to the destination denoted by the large color first, then to another destination denoted by the smaller swatch. Letters can designate towns or spots. Andy Sperandeo photo

Fig. 6-7 (above right): Jim Hediger used the conductor's wheel report concept to make a matrix that shows each town along the left and each car type (by AAR code) along the top. The yardmaster can make up the train by totaling the car types, and road crews can switch towns by swapping like types of cars. Jim Hediger photo

PC-based system that allows you to make and customize your own forms. Additional sources of car-forwarding information, paperwork, or software, including some powerful and data-packed software systems, are listed in the Appendix.

Four-cycle waybills

Now that we've established a reasonable case for car

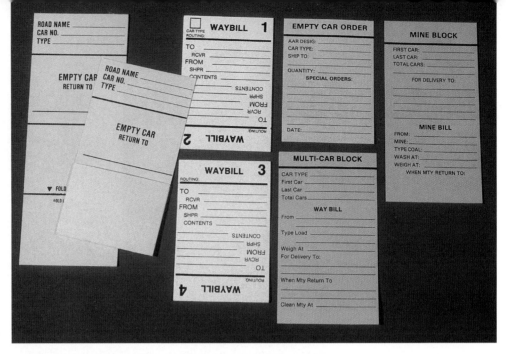

Fig. 6-8: Four-cycle waybills and associated forms are produced by Old Line Graphics. A flap on each car card (at left) is folded up and taped to form a pocket that shows only one of the four waybill cycles. Empty car orders (with special overlay waybills printed on the back) route empties to customers. The mine block and multi-car forms allow a block of cars to be shipped on one waybill.

Fig. 6-9: This diagram shows how a four-cycle waybill can be used to route a car (A) from west staging to an on-line shipper, back to staging, then over the entire railroad and back; (B) back and forth over your railroad to simulate bridge traffic; (C) from staging to staging, back to an on-line shopper, back to east staging, then back to west staging; (D) back and forth from an on-line industry to east staging in captive service; (E) on-line industry to west staging, then to east staging, the back to west staging and, finally, to the original shipper; and so on. A car coming onto the railroad via an interchange would make the same moves as one coming out of a hidden staging yard.

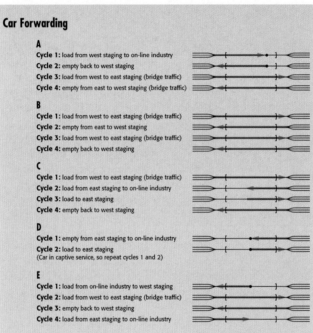

Car Forwarding

A
Cycle 1: load from west staging to on-line industry
Cycle 2: empty back to west staging
Cycle 3: load from west to east staging (bridge traffic)
Cycle 4: empty from east to west staging (bridge traffic)

B
Cycle 1: load from west to east staging (bridge traffic)
Cycle 2: empty from east to west staging
Cycle 3: load from west to east staging (bridge traffic)
Cycle 4: empty back to west staging

C
Cycle 1: load from west to east staging (bridge traffic)
Cycle 2: load east staging to on-line industry
Cycle 3: load to east staging
Cycle 4: empty back to west staging

D
Cycle 1: empty from east staging to on-line industry
Cycle 2: load to east staging
(Car in captive service, so repeat cycles 1 and 2)

E
Cycle 1: load from on-line industry to west staging
Cycle 2: load from west to east staging (bridge traffic)
Cycle 3: empty back to west staging
Cycle 4: load from east staging to on-line industry

cards and waybills, let's look at how they're prepared and used. Setting up any system can seem overwhelming if you don't break it down into easy steps, so let's focus on just one car. Once you master the basics, you can crank out car cards and waybills by the dozen while you're watching TV or relaxing on the porch, or even while killing time on a business trip.

The idea is to cause a car to move in a purposeful manner without you having to do a lot of paperwork

prior to each session. This system lets you do the paperwork up front, once, and then merely cycle the waybills. Special "overlay" forms, which we'll discuss shortly, allow many variations to the basic routine established by four-cycle waybills.

The original system utilized 3″ x 5″ cards with a clear-plastic pocket taped to one end. Waybills were often used once, then returned to a master file. The original system still has its advocates, but four-cycle car cards and

waybills have many advantages, in my view: smaller size (2″ x 4″) of the car cards into which the waybill is inserted, fold-up waybill pocket (no separate "window" needs to be cut and attached), four car-movement cycles (rather than one or two), and many supporting forms such as multi-car-block waybills, empty-car order forms that simulate the call between customer and agent or agent and yardmaster, special overlay waybills, and so on (fig. 6-8).

A waybill is inserted into the folded-up pocket on each car card. This allows the user to see only the top half of one side of the waybill. After that cycle is completed, the layout owner turns the waybill upside down to expose the bottom of the front of the waybill with instructions for the next movement. This is typically done between operating sessions. (Asking crews to remember to cycle waybills is highly problematic, not realistic, and not recommended. "Read and heed" is all that crew members should be expected to do.)

When cycle 2 has been finished, the layout owner flips the waybill over between sessions to expose cycles 3 and (a session, or "day," later) cycle 4. This means the waybill does not cycle back to position 1 until the fifth operating session. By then, the repetitive nature of the four cycles won't be apparent, so the waybill usually never needs to be removed from the car card. This avoids the hassle of trying to match loose waybills to the proper car types and road names to ensure Car Service Rules are observed.

In some cases, only cycles

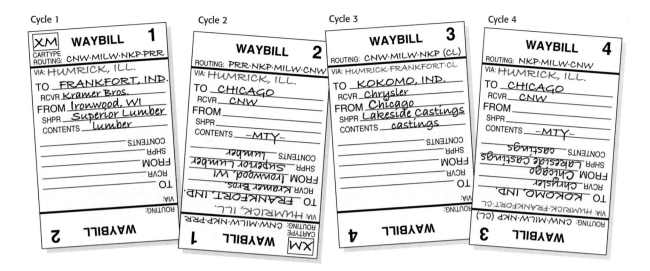

Cycle 1

| XM | WAYBILL | **1** |

CARTYPE
ROUTING: *CNW·MILW·NKP·PRR*
VIA: *HUMRICK, ILL.*
TO *FRANKFORT, IND.*
RCVR *Kramer Bros.*
FROM *Ironwood, WI*
SHPR *Superior Lumber*
CONTENTS *Lumber*

Cycle 2

| | WAYBILL | **2** |

ROUTING: *PRR·NKP·MILW·CNW*
VIA: *HUMRICK, ILL.*
TO *CHICAGO*
RCVR *CNW*
FROM
SHPR
CONTENTS *—MTY—*

Cycle 3

| | WAYBILL | **3** |

ROUTING: *CNW·MILW·NKP (CL)*
VIA: *HUMRICK·FRANKFORT·CL*
TO *KOKOMO, IND.*
RCVR *Chrysler*
FROM *Chicago*
SHPR *Lakeside Castings*
CONTENTS *castings*

Cycle 4

| | WAYBILL | **4** |

ROUTING: *NKP·MILW·CNW*
VIA: *HUMRICK, ILL.*
TO *CHICAGO*
RCVR *CNW*
FROM
SHPR
CONTENTS *—MTY—*

Fig. 6-10: The four cycles needed to move a C&NW boxcar from Wisconsin to Frankfort, Ind., back to the C&NW, then to Kokomo, Ind. (off the modeled part of the NKP east of Frankfort), and then home again are shown here. The Via line shows that the car enters and leaves the NKP's Third Subdivision via the Milwaukee Road interchange at Humrick, Ill., rather than the west-end staging yard. It reaches Kokomo, Ind., via the Clover Leaf District east-end staging yard (fig. 6-11).

1 and 2 will be used. A surprising number of freight cars are used in repetitive, "captive-service" traffic patterns. A boxcar equipped with special loading racks for, say, automobile transmissions might cycle back and forth between an automobile transmission plant in Kokomo, Ind., and a Detroit assembly plant for years.

By the numbers: waybill cycles

Let's walk through an entire car-movement cycle, step-by-step, so you can understand how the four-cycle waybill system works. In the process, you'll also gain insights into the way full-size railroads manage car movements. We'll use the Third Subdivision of the Nickel Plate Road's St. Louis Division of the Clover Leaf District for this exercise, mainly because I'm modeling it and have compiled a lot of information useful for our purposes. Railroad names from the mid-1950s, the period I'm modeling, will be used here.

We'll first look at a simple four-cycle example, then add some bells and whistles. As shown in fig. 6-9, you can route cars in a variety of ways by properly using each of the four waybill cycles. A car can bounce back and forth between staging yards at either end of your railroad, for example, thus nicely emulating overhead or "bridge" traffic.

Let's use the scheme shown in fig. 6-9A, where a car begins its sequence of moves over a railroad by coming out of a staged interchange.

Cycle 1: Cars are never loaded in a yard, so you can't start a load-empty cycle there. Let's therefore assume that the car in question is a Chicago & North Western boxcar loaded with lumber by the Superior Lumber Co. in Ironwood, Wis.

I don't know the name of an actual sawmill in northern Wisconsin, so I made one up after looking at a Rand-McNally railroad atlas and spotting Ironwood on a C&NW line. If a visiting modeler who knows better provides an actual mill's name and location, I can thank him or her and fill out a new waybill. Or a review of the Operations SIG's massive shipper database (see Appendix) might uncover a suitable shipper.

The car is destined for Kramer Bros. lumber yard on the Pennsylvania Railroad in Frankfort, Ind., an actual destination. We can now fill out the to and from parts of cycle 1 of a waybill.

How do we route the car? We know the C&NW (Union Pacific today) serves Ironwood and, as its name implies, that it ends in Chicago. The atlas shows several railroads out of the Windy City that head south toward Frankfort in west-central Indiana. We'll assume the Milwaukee Road sales staff wined and dined the sawmill's owner, so they get a part of the line haul. The MILW can hand it off to the NKP at Cheneyville or Humrick, Ill. We'll use the Via line to specify that the car is routed to the NKP's St. Louis Div. via Humrick. The NKP will interchange it with the Pennsy in Frankfort. So the routing line will show CNW-MILW-NKP-PRR (fig. 6-10).

What do we do to get the billed car moving? Since the routing line says the NKP gets the car from the Milwaukee Road, and since the part of the NKP I'm modeling interchanges with the MILW at Humrick, Ill., let's put it on the interchange track at Humrick.

But the Pennsy crosses the Third Sub at both Frankfort, Ind., and Oakland, Ill. To which PRR interchange should the car go—west to Oakland or east to Frankfort? The destination—to Frankfort—solves this riddle, so the next eastbound that works Humrick will take the car (and its car card and waybill) on east to Frankfort. Humrick is a very important interchange point—in 1953, the NKP received 12,000 loads there!—so the car will be picked up within a few hours.

When the train arrives in Frankfort yard, the yardmaster sees "PRR" on the routing

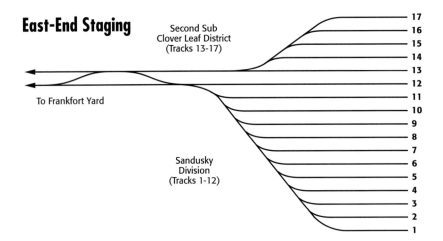

East-End Staging

Second Sub
Clover Leaf District
(Tracks 13-17)

To Frankfort Yard

Sandusky
Division
(Tracks 1-12)

17
16
15
14
13
12
11
10
9
8
7
6
5
4
3
2
1

Fig. 6-11: This schematic diagram of the author's east-end staging yards shows why the yardmaster needs to know whether a car is going into a train headed east on the Sandusky Division (tracks 1-12) or northeast on the Second Sub of the Clover Leaf Dist. (tracks 13-17).

line as the railroad that gets the car from the NKP. The yard crew cuts off the car and later shoves it into the PRR interchange. Between sessions, the car is presumed to have been delivered to Kramer Lumber by the PRR and unloaded, then returned to the NKP interchange for routing home to the C&NW. The waybill is therefore cycled by turning it upside down to show this.

Cycle 2: The car is now shown to be unloaded (fig. 6-10). By Association of American Railroads (AAR) Car Service Rules, it must be routed back to home rails by the same route it traversed when loaded. The routing line therefore shows PRR-NKP-MILW-CNW, and the Via line shows "Humrick, Ill."

The "Via" line is an important enhancement to waybills suggested by Harold Werthwein. Harold models the Delaware Division of the Erie in the transition era, including many long branches. While local crews quickly mastered the location of towns on the main line, they weren't sure what to do with cars destined for lesser-known branch towns. Which branch were they on? Harold's solution was to add the Via line and note the junction on the main line

where branch cars should be set out.

Specifying "via Humrick" for a car routed from the MILW and NKP to the PRR is an extension of that usage. The yardmaster therefore has the car picked up and put in no. 45, the West Local, for delivery to the Milwaukee interchange at Humrick, a move the West Local crew makes every day and therefore clearly understands.

Cycle 3: The car is once again sitting on the MILW interchange at Humrick as the session ends. The waybill must therefore reflect this location when it is cycled, between sessions, by turning it over to reveal position 3 (fig. 6-10). We'll assume that, between sessions, the car went home to the C&NW, was loaded with automatic-transmission castings in Chicago, and was sent back down to the NKP via the MILW at Humrick for delivery to a Chrysler transmission plant in Kokomo, Ind.

The routing is similar: CNW-MILW-NKP via Humrick. The car is picked up at Humrick, taken east to Frankfort, and put on an eastbound local to Kokomo —which is to say, into the east-end staging yard.

But hold on a moment:

The NKP map (fig. 2-4) shows that there are two mainline routes east of Frankfort: the former Clover Leaf main to Toledo, O., and the former Lake Erie & Western main to Lima and Sandusky, O. So which eastbound division local gets the car?

Kokomo is on the former Clover Leaf, and the Via line tells the yardmaster to put it on a Toledo Division, rather than a Sandusky Division, local by showing "Via Frankfort (Clover Leaf)." That's important, as the yardmaster may not have a clue as to which line Kokomo is on. After all, it's represented by just another staging track. Which staging tracks (13–17) are designated for Clover Leaf District trains and which are reserved for Sandusky Division trains (1–12) is shown by a nearby diagram (fig. 6-11), although I usually pre-assign regular trains to specific staging tracks.

Cycle 4: Between sessions, the waybill is turned upside down to show position 4 (fig. 6-10). That causes the C&NW boxcar to be routed from Clover Leaf east-end staging through Frankfort back to the Milwaukee Road via Humrick. Between sessions, when cycle 1 is once again revealed, the car will be perfectly positioned to deliver another load of Wisconsin

lumber to Kramer via the PRR at Frankfort. By then, Kramer Bros. should be starving for more lumber.

Moreover, no one will be bothered by having a "plain-vanilla" C&NW boxcar show up again five sessions later. (Let's hear it for unremarkable, freight-car-red, 40-foot boxcars!) The waybill can therefore stay with that car indefinitely.

Now that we've worked through a four-cycle movement of a typical boxcar, let's up the ante a bit by using that empty C&NW boxcar more efficiently.

Empty cars

Car Service Rules (CSRs) adopted by the Association of American Railroads specify that the railroads sharing in the revenues derived from moving a load to its destination must also share in the cost of returning the car back to home rails as an empty (often abbreviated "MT" or "MTY"). So an MTY car is typically reverse-routed home, retracing every mile of its outbound journey.

To avoid moving a lot of empty cars around, which would hurt efficient car utilization, another CSR says that a railroad should load a foreign-road car if (1) the load is heading back toward, to, or beyond the Home

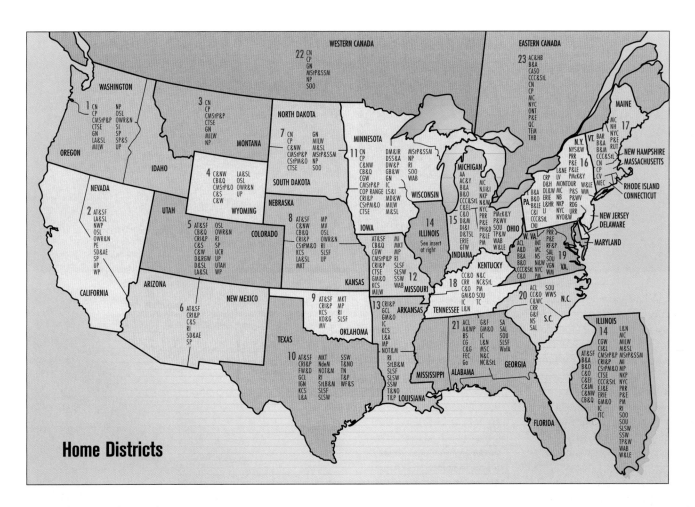

Home Districts

District (see map, fig. 6-12) of the car's owner, and (2) the car is suitable for that type of lading. So the NKP could load an empty Maine Central boxcar with appliances if it were a clean, tight boxcar and the destination were toward or in New England, but it couldn't load a Florida East Coast or Spokane, Portland & Seattle boxcar and send it to that destination.

Capturing a suitable empty for loading is easily accomplished using an Old Line Graphics green empty-car order form and the special waybill form on its reverse side. Those forms each represent a call from a shipper to the railroad's local agent.

Let's assume the manager of the Thompson grain elevator in Cayuga, Ind., called NKP agent Mitchell to tell him the elevator needs an empty boxcar for loading with grain tomorrow. Mr.

Fig. 6-12: Home Region map

Fig. 6-13: The Old Line Graphics empty-car order form is used to simulate a call from a customer to the agent, and then from the agent to the yardmaster. It is slipped into a car card on top of the existing waybill to capture an empty car for loading. After the car has been spotted, the form is flipped over to show a special waybill routing the car to a new destination. Care must be used to match the destination and car's home region according to Car Service Rules (fig. 6-12).

Mitchell then calls the yardmaster in Frankfort, Ind., to tell him what he'll need on tomorrow's local.

Cycle 1: To illustrate how we can locate a suitable foreign-road empty boxcar, per the Car Service Rules, for loading with grain, we'll start

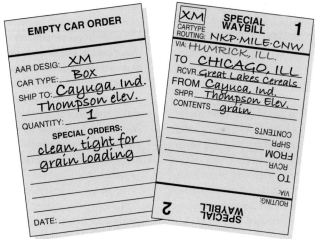

out the same way with a C&NW boxcar containing a load of lumber for Kramer Bros. on the PRR at Frankfort. As before, it's delivered to the PRR interchange at Frankfort, per waybill cycle 1.

Cycle 2: "Tomorrow"—the next operating session—the Frankfort yard crew working the PRR interchange finds

the C&NW boxcar with its waybill cycled to position 2. This shows the car as an empty for the C&NW at Chicago. As before, the West Local could deliver it back to the Milwaukee Road at Humrick for forwarding to the C&NW. If, however, the yardmaster needs empties for loading, he may "capture" it en route.

When the yardmaster reports for his work shift, or "trick," he typically finds a stack of these forms. They generate a demand for empty boxcars based on how many on-line industries there are on this division making such "requests." The top form happens to be the one from agent Mitchell at Cayuga (fig. 6-13).

These empty-car order forms are made out in advance of the first operating session and left where the yardmaster will find them. They can be reused indefinitely to generate requests for empty cars, so filling out the forms ("taking the messages") is usually done only once unless new traffic-originating industries are added to the railroad.

Per AAR Car Service Rules, the YM tries to find foreign-road empties that can be loaded and sent toward home rails. Failing that, he uses home-road cars from a stash usually kept on a yard track for this purpose, especially during the grain-rush seasons (summer for winter wheat, fall for corn and soy beans).

He notices the empty C&NW boxcar picked up from the Pennsy and compares it to the empty-car order. On the back of this form is a special waybill

Fig. 6-14 (above): The Western Maryland's East Local, photographed just east of Parsons, W. Va., in May 1974, has wood-chip cars cut in at the head end to avoid contaminating them with coal dust. (Wood chips in the coal are less of a concern.) Use job aids such as instruction cards given to local crews or placards posted at the industry or yard to enforce such practices on a model railroad (above right).

Fig. 6-15: Covered hoppers were spotted at this ammonium-nitrate unloader on the South Branch Valley in W. Va. (right), a small industry the author modeled by using a cement-silo kit (below right). The chemical is used to make mine blasting powder.

that's already made out (fig. 6-13), so he can determine quickly whether this empty is suitable for that load.

The waybill is "special" in that it overlays, and hence covers up, the existing waybill and reroutes the car. (The regular waybill remains in the car card.) The yardmaster notes that the special waybill will route the car to a customer in Chicago, a Home District for the C&NW according to the AAR map, so he slides the green empty-car order form into the

Passenger Car and Load Demand Cards

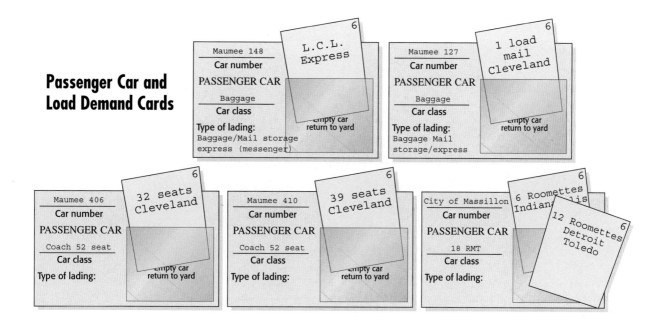

Maumee 148	L.C.L. Express 6
Car number	
PASSENGER CAR	
Baggage	
Car class	
Type of lading: Baggage/Mail storage express (messenger)	Empty car return to yard

Maumee 127	1 load mail Cleveland 6
Car number	
PASSENGER CAR	
Baggage	
Car class	
Type of lading: Baggage Mail storage/express	Empty car return to yard

Maumee 406	32 seats Cleveland 6
Car number	
PASSENGER CAR	
Coach 52 seat	
Car class	
Type of lading:	Empty car return to yard

Maumee 410	39 seats Cleveland 6
Car number	
PASSENGER CAR	
Coach 52 seat	
Car class	
Type of lading:	Empty car return to yard

City of Massillon	6 Roomettes Indian... is 6 · 12 Roomettes Detroit Toledo 6
Car number	
PASSENGER CAR	
18 RMT	
Car class	
Type of lading:	

pocket in front of the regular waybill, thus concealing the latter from view.

The C&NW boxcar is then switched in the proper sequence into the West Local's consist, along with any other MTYs requested by agents in other towns along the Third Sub (more empty-car order forms). The MTYs join any cars with waybills showing them to be loads routed to those towns.

When the local has spotted the C&NW boxcar on the elevator track, the elevator can then load it with grain. Elevator workers have to nail "grain doors" inside the boxcar door openings so the grain won't run out as fast as it is piped in. An occasional boxcar-load of grain doors is another source of rail traffic to a grain elevator.

Between operating sessions, the form is turned over to reveal the special waybill side. The local then picks up the C&NW and takes it one town farther west to Humrick, as the "Via" line shows, where it is turned over to the Milwaukee Road for the trip to Chicago.

Also between sessions, the special waybill is removed, turned over, and left where

the Frankfort yardmaster will find it to create a demand for another empty at Thompson's elevator in Cayuga. This time the empty box spotted there will almost certainly be a different one, as the C&NW boxcar is unlikely to be the first one at hand when the empty-car order surfaces.

Removing the special waybill uncovers the original, permanent waybill still set at cycle 2 (fig. 6-10). It is then cycled to be in agreement with the car's location on the Milwaukee interchange at Humrick as another load bound for a destination on or reached via the NKP. Having several C&NW boxcars appear on the railroad via the Humrick interchange helps disguise the repetitive movements of any one car.

Car placement in trains

If you were an engineer or conductor, would you want a tank car filled with a highly flammable liquid coupled next to the locomotive or caboose? ICC (now FRA) regulations therefore require such cars to be placed at least 5 cars behind the engine and ahead of the caboose, or centered in the consist in shorter trains.

Loads of ammonium nitrate were considered hazardous cargo when they were billed to a customer who would use it to make mine blasting powder (fig. 6-15), but they were treated as loads of plain old fertilizer when billed to a farm supplier. That rule was changed, as it could burn or explode if mixed with diesel fuel following a derailment.

Practical considerations led to other car-placement rules. Car loads of wood chips, for example, could be contaminated by the "whiffle dust" coming off loaded hoppers (fig. 6-14). Lighter cars, such as empty piggy-back flats, can "string-line" (pull off the rails toward the center of the curve) when they're at the head end of a heavy train, be they full-size cars or simply models.

Passenger train forms

The typical passenger train, if there ever was such a thing, had baggage and railway post office cars on the head-end, followed by coaches, a diner, and sleepers. The diner could thus be reached by coach passengers without their traipsing through the first-class

Fig. 6-16: Bill Darnaby created cards representing the demand for coach seats and sleeper berths for his Maumee Route. If demand exceeds capacity, another car needs to be added.

accommodations. There were also all-coach trains and all first-class trains.

Where things get interesting, as a rule, is in a major city. There head-end cars will be cut off or added to the consist, and an extra coach or sleeper may be tacked on as well. Another spot where switching occurs is at a major split in a railroad's main line, with one line headed for, say, Chicago, the other to St. Louis.

If you're modeling a prototype, car adds and drops may be all worked out for you, but such operations could vary as demand rose or fell. Bill Darnaby therefore worked out a load-demand card system (fig. 6-16). These cards specify the number of coach seats sold or the number of sleeping berths sold by type (bedroom, roomette, etc.). If the demand for seats or berths exceeds the train's normal complement, more cars have to be added before

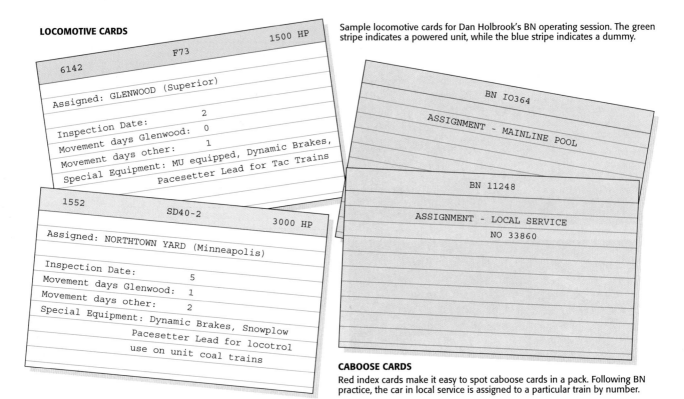

Sample locomotive cards for Dan Holbrook's BN operating session. The green stripe indicates a powered unit, while the blue stripe indicates a dummy.

CABOOSE CARDS

Red index cards make it easy to spot caboose cards in a pack. Following BN practice, the car in local service is assigned to a particular train by number.

departure. The same procedures apply to head-end cars.

Bill described his system in detail on pages 74-77 of October 1993 *Model Railroader*.

Locomotive and caboose cards

Dan Holbrook described a way of adding more realism to his railroad's operation in the February 1992 MR (pages 122-123): 3 x 5 cards that allow locomotives and cabooses to be handled as they would be on full-size railroads.

He filled out a car for each locomotive (fig. 6-17). The color stripe atop a loco card indicates whether it's a powered or dummy unit. The numbers such as "inspection date" represent operating sessions. F7B 6142 is due for inspection at Glenwood, its assigned district, on session 2, and the "movement days: 0" shows that it doesn't have to be moved to Glenwood for inspection, as it's assigned there. If it's assigned somewhere else, the "other" movement day of 1 tells when it

has to be started toward Glenwood. This mimics the 30-, 60-, and 90-day federal inspection intervals in the 1970s, which Dan's Burlington Northern depicts. This routes locomotives just as waybills route freight cars, although with much less frequency.

In the 1970s, Dan reported, BN was still assigning cabooses to specific locals or freights. The caboose cards show what service each caboose has been assigned to. So yard crews can't simply pull the first caboose off the caboose track and stick it on the valley local, as it may be assigned to road service. You could up the ante by assigning cabooses to specific conductors, as was done in the steam era, and then trying to figure out how to match your regular operators to cabooses. I'm still scratching my head on that one.

Special forms

The Old Line Graphics package includes forms for unit trains and multi-car

blocks, such as a block of reefers that will travel together over your railroad. Why bother making out individual waybills when a number of cars, or an entire train, won't be switched on your part of the rail network? On the Allegheny Midland, we shipped cuts of hoppers to single destinations using mine-block forms.

Old Line also sells pads of bad-order tickets, which can be used to mark cars for attention between sessions. Other forms include green car cards for passenger equipment and red ones for cabooses (the standard cards are a buff color).

Moving coal

One lump of soft coal looks pretty much like another, but in terms of their chemical composition they may be significantly different. A mine that produces coal with a high sulfur content will have a different customer base than a low-sulfur coal producer. Coal is also graded by size (see fig. 5-7)

Fig. 6-17: Dan Holbrook uses cards to coordinate the use and servicing of locomotives as well as caboose assignments. The number after the inspection date tells when the unit needs to be started toward its home base for inspection. The caboose cards show specific train assignments. In the steam era, each caboose was assigned to a specific conductor, who regarded it as his home away from home.

for use in locomotive fireboxes, home furnaces, steel mills, coking plants, power plants, and so on.

Coal loaded at a simple truck dump (fig. 5-5) is typically run-of-mine coal and is either sold as such or is taken to a preparation plant for cleaning and sizing. Larger truck dumps have some crushing and cleaning machinery built into them (fig. 5-6). Anthracite cleaning plants, called breakers or collieries, tended to be very large buildings.

A coal prep plant usually

Fig. 6-18: This mine ticket from the Montour RR in Pennsylvania shows that Bessemer & Lake Erie hopper 95865 is being routed from Westland Mine 162 to Champion, Pa.

Fig. 6-19: They may all look alike, but coal loads are switched very much like general merchandise to assure that coal of the desired size and chemical composition reaches each customer. This sea of coal was waiting to continue its eastward trek from the Chessie System's ex-Baltimore & Ohio yard at Keyser, W. Va., in June 1976.

loaded only one size of coal per track. For the modeler, this means that each track under a large tipple ships a different product to a different customer. It's as though track 1 shipped paper, track 2 bricks, track 3 beer, and so on. Mine billing tickets (fig. 6-18) need to show whether the coal must be sent elsewhere for cleaning or weighing, and the end customer for that cut of hoppers. This will help yard crews assemble the right grades and sizes of coal into trains (fig. 6-19).

I discussed coal operations at length in the February 1997 Model Railroader. If you're modeling a coal road, be sure to read David Morgan's benchmark article, "Tide 470," in the April 1956 Trains. This story describes how the C&O orchestrated the movement of various types of coal to tidewater so that a ship could be loaded with the desired mix of coal and sail on a specific date.

Car "rental" fees

Railroads try to get foreign-road cars off their rails before midnight, when the daily per-diem charge is calculated, by making a "midnight shove" into an interchange track. Perhaps not surprisingly, two railroads in a major city that were rushing to beat the deadline simultaneously executed this supposedly money-saving maneuver on the same interchange track with unfortunate consequences.

Customers who receive loaded cars are given several days to unload the cars before rental charges, called demurrage, are incurred. Such charges are nominal, but they encourage more efficient use of the car fleet. For some customers, however, the charges are low enough for them to regard freight cars as mobile warehouses; paying demurrage may be cheaper than building a new warehouse!

To increase the size of the car fleet, in the 1970s car per-diem charges were substantially increased for newly built, railroad-owned cars only. The high fees attracted outside investors, who contracted with short lines to "borrow" their reporting marks. The result was car fleets that, if coupled together, were longer than the short line itself! When the demand for such expensive cars later fell and those cars came back to "home" rails, serious congestion often resulted. For the modeler, however, the wide variety of colorful paint schemes on 50-foot boxcars of that era added a lot of visual interest.

Such concerns rarely affect model operations, as we tend to move cars the next "day" just to keep the action levels up. But some enterprising operator has almost certainly found a way to work such concerns into his or her railroad's operating scheme, or soon will.

That's the beauty of operation: It's always evolving, and many of you who are just learning about it here will one day make your own "contributions to the literature."

CHAPTER SEVEN
Moving trains

Fig. 7-1: If you enjoy switching out on the main line, running the local is where the action often is. Here an Allegheny Midland Mike sets out a carload of kaolin, used to coat "enameled" paper, on the Western Maryland interchange track at North Durbin, W. Va.

Most of us became interested in model railroading because of the action. Our model trains can do pretty much everything that their full-size prototypes do or did, thanks to a pair of rails, wheels with flanges, and some electrical wizardry. The main purpose of this book is to show you ways to enhance those actions by giving our trains and the crews that run them specific work to do. Let's examine what it is we're trying to emulate: the types of trains, and then ways to move them safely and efficiently. Then we'll discuss ways to "model" those systems, and the advantages and pitfalls of each.

Fig. 7-2 (left): Locals aren't necessarily short trains pulled by a single engine. If there's a lot of work to do on that division, three or more units may be up front. Here a trio of Western Maryland F units sets out a boxcar at Parsons, W. Va. , in May 1973.

Freight trains

Local or way freights: For many modelers, this is where the action is as local freights (also called way freights, peddlers, drills, patrols, and by a host of other colorful monikers) switched towns along the main line (fig. 7-1). Their role is to do most of the en route pick ups and set outs to minimize delays to through and fast freights on each division of the railroad.

The part of the Nickel Plate I'm modeling ran only one local each day, and it ran westbound as a second-class freight, no. 45. It typically stopped at every town on the division, dropping off inbound cars and picking up outbounds. Its timetable status as a second-class westbound train meant that it had to clear all first-class trains (passenger trains 9 and 10) and all eastbound second-class through

and fast freights, as eastbound trains were superior to westbounds on the NKP. But no train orders had to be issued on its behalf under normal circumstances.

Eastbound cars were handled either by moving them to a town farther west where an eastbound through freight had to stop anyway to work an important interchange, or by hauling them on west to the next division-point yard. There they were switched into the consist of an eastbound freight. The local's crew, engine, and caboose returned home on an eastbound freight after they got their legally required rest period.

If the work load warranted, other divisions of the NKP and many other railroads ran locals in both directions. Crews on both locals cooperated to mini-

Fig. 7-3 (above left): Smaller railroads usually survive by offering a higher level of personal attention to customers. In August 1972, the Green Mountain switched a talc plant—a good example of a small regional industry—at Gassetts, Vt., on the former Rutland line between Rutland and Bellows Falls.

Fig. 7-4 (above): The Nickel Plate's Gibson City (Ill.) Turn heads back east to Frankfort, Ind., as it crosses the Wabash River at Lafayette. A pair of GP30s was common power on this train. NKP units were renumbered by putting a 2 in front of the road number following the October 16, 1964, merger with the N&W; 907 became 2907.

mize runaround moves to switch facing-point spurs where possible. Some railroads ran "turn-around" locals, which typically met in the middle of a division, swapped crews, and then continued their runs. This allowed crews to get back to their home terminals each night, which was better—and cheaper—for all concerned.

Locals aren't necessarily short trains. They may look like through freights pulled by several units (fig. 7-2).

Conversely, on short lines a through freight may look and act like a local, as there simply isn't enough traffic to warrant both, or customer-service concerns demand more personalized attention (fig. 7-3).

Extras and sections: Through and fast freights, and sometimes locals, often have published schedules, usually as second- or third-class trains. Trains not listed in the timetable are operated

as extra freights and work extras. The lead locomotive must carry white flags (fig. 7-5) or classification lights to alert trains it meets and passes of its extra status. Additional traffic can also be moved by running one or more sections of a scheduled train, with all sections except the last carrying green flags or class lights.

Turns: If there's enough interchange with a major crossing railroad or traffic to or from a major customer, a railroad may operate a "turn" to that point. A turn is typically a freight that heads out from a yard to a specific point short of the next division-point yard, sets out and/or picks up important cars for or from a major industry or crossing railroad, and then returns to its point of origin, hence its name (fig. 7-4). One division of the Texas & Pacific (UP today) ran three turns each day, except Sunday, to handle the traffic!

Through freights: Yards would quickly become plugged if freights weren't regularly dispatched. Cars of "dead freight" of low priority are usually moved in through freights from one division-

point yard to the next (fig. 7-6). Such trains are blocked with "propers" for the next yard and "throughs" for points beyond that yard. They may also have hot cars for interchanges on their division blocked on the head end so they can make a quick set-out at important cross-ings with foreign lines. This ensures much more rapid movement of important mer-chandise such as perishables (fruit and vegetables), beer, and auto parts than could be accomplished by having it picked up or set out by a daily local.

Fast freights: Some trains comprise only a single block or a very few blocks. The Texas & Pacific's *Fruit Block* is an example. The train was

blocked at its point of origin and hustled to its destination or the railroad that handled the next leg as fast as the railroad could manage. As little switching as possible was done at division-point yards en route to avoid delays. Yard switching can consume incredible amounts of time, so pre-blocked through trains can maintain much faster schedules.

Even a fast freight may have some "shorts" on one end for the yard switcher to cut off (fig. 1-2). A block of hot "throughs" may then be tacked on, along with a new caboose for the next division's crew. (In the steam era, cabooses were often assigned to conductors and went wherever they went, and not

a moment before.) Mean-while, the road engine is being serviced or replaced, and reefers on the head end are being iced. This entire process could be done in well under an hour.

Railroads such as the Nickel Plate that depended on overhead or bridge traffic, as opposed to those that originated or terminated a lot of traffic, lived and died by the clock. NKP management knew that connections had to be made or traffic managers would route their meat and produce on a rival railroad such as the Wabash. If a local crew left a mainline switch open or a through freight didn't clear up in time, thus "sticking" a hot eastbound such as KC-44 out of St.

Louis or OB-2 out of Chicago (Osborn, Ill.), they'd hear about it with certain swiftness and little subtlety.

The key was to quickly combine like blocks on two or more symbol freights so those hot freights could continue their daily races to eastern markets. NKP's no. 98, carrying symbol MB-98, was a hot eastbound out of St. Louis (Madison, Ill.) that began its run toward Buffalo at 11 a.m. each day. Half an hour later, no. 62 (PB-2) started its eastbound trek out of Peoria, Ill. MB-98 arrived in Frankfort, Ind., at 7 p.m., PB-2 15 minutes later. Part of MB-98 formed the nucleus of FT-98 to Toledo, and PB-2 was merged into MB-98 for a 7:30 p.m. departure. At the NKP's hub

in Bellevue, O., MB-98 was again split to form the basis for one of the hot Alpha Jets, AJ-2, that ran east over several partnering railroads while 98 continued east to Buffalo. No excuses were accepted for delaying 98 at either Frankfort or Bellevue despite the switching that occurred there.

So don't regard yard switching as a mind-numbing chore whereby every car in the yard is sorted one at a time. Locals may be built that way, as are parts of through freights, but often entire blocks of cars are switched as units. A block of loaded reefers heading east from California or north from Florida is a good example. There can be real action and drama in a yard as crews

anticipate the arrival of hot freights, then do everything in their power to get them out of town again as expeditiously as possible.

Symbol freights: Image-enhancing names and symbols are often applied to fast freights by the railroad's marketing and sales divisions to gain an edge in highly competitive markets. Telling a potential customer that his precious cargo will be forwarded on the *Fruit Block, Blue Streak,* or *Florida Perishable* (figs. 1-4 and 3-5) sounds more impressive than saying it will be routed on train 261.

Not all hot trains were named. The NKP's legendary string of hot eastbounds carried symbols such as MB-98 (Madison, near St. Louis, to

Buffalo), KC-44 (forwarding reefers from Kansas City), and CB-12 (Chicago to Buffalo). On many railroads, management worried more about a delayed symbol freight than a tardy passenger train, as moving high-rate freight was where most of their profits came from.

To a railroader, however, the train number is what's important. MB-98 usually ran on no. 98's schedule, but any eastbound freight could have been designated as MB-98 if so needed to meet advertised schedules. Train orders would refer to "No 98," not "MB-98." (More on train orders shortly.)

Mine runs: These are the equivalent of a local freight on a mine branch. Swapping empties for loads requires just as much put-and-take (fig. 7-7) as switching any other industry, as the type and/or size of coal loaded into each cut of hoppers has to be dealt with as a separate commodity. Mine runs, also called shifters, also serve the function of local freights by hauling LCL (less than carload lot) freight, mine supplies, and other occasional merchandise loads (fig. 7-8).

Passenger trains

Passenger trains may set the theme of operation for your entire railroad or simply add some measure of class and cadence. Like freights, they came in many "flavors." Some were accorded only a number, whereas others such as Santa Fe's *Super Chief*, Pennsy's *Broadway Limited*, and New York Central's *20th Century* Limited became stars of stage and screen. Some smaller railroads also operated notable trains—the Monon's *Thoroughbreds* and the Delaware & Hudson's *Laurentians* behind ex-Santa Fe PAs (fig. 7-9) come readily to mind.

Some of those names were continued after Amtrak took over most passenger trains in the United States in May 1971. Such trains were usually perennial money losers, but they played a role in marketing the railroad's profitable freight services.

Like freights, passenger trains could be operated in sections or as extras simply by issuing train orders to that effect. The lead locomotives had to display the proper signals—green flags or classification lights to indicate another section was following, white for extras (fig. 7-10)—to alert crews they met and passed as to their special status. Lead sections also blew a long and two shorts to call attention to the following section.

Railroads operated passenger counterparts of their local freights that stopped in each town. Although speed suffered, convenience increased. On some lines where passengers were few and far between, railroads operated "mixed" trains, with passengers carried in a coach or combine, often tacked onto the rear of the train, or even in the caboose. Short lines were famous for such trains, which prompted the classic book *Mixed Train Daily* by Lucius Beebe and Charles Clegg.

Orchestrating train movements

As soon as the second locomotive was built, the potential for a collision existed. In the early days, it was relatively easy to manage a limited number of trains, but keeping a path clear between stations soon became a formal job. Over the years, train dispatching evolved into highly sophisticated systems, yet even today trains are moved efficiently and safely using some very simple procedures requiring nothing more than paper forms, pens or pencils, and two-way radios.

I'll start by reviewing systems that a number of modelers have used with success, then delve into an increasingly popular way to orchestrate train movements: timetable and train-order operation.

Centralized Traffic Control (CTC): A highly efficient traffic control system, often used on single-track mains, is called Centralized Traffic Control, or CTC. Introduced in the 1930s and widely implemented in the 1940s, CTC allowed a dispatcher to control train movements at a console (fig. 7-11) simply by flipping a few levers that established the desired direction of the movement and set switch points to facilitate that move, then pushing a button. The systems' internal workings then displayed the proper signal indications (see Chapter 8) while preventing conflicting routes from being set up. Signal indications supersede the superiority of trains in CTC territory, so all trains operate like extras without regard to timetable authority.

When crews need to work locally, they can request "track and time" from the dispatcher, who can then authorize them to work by saying, for example, "Track and time limits granted 1:01 p.m. to 2:15 p.m. on the main between east and west switches of siding at Fostoria." The local crew can

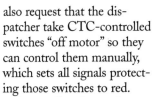

Fig. 7-11 (above): A CTC panel helped the dispatcher manage David Barrow's Cat Mountain & Santa Fe from a room directly below the railroad. The olive green center section denotes a Union Switch & Signal-style panel, whereas General Railway Signal panels were typically all black. Tommy Holt photo

Fig. 7-12 (above right): Michigantown, Ind., was on the NKP's Clover Leaf Dist. in manual-block territory. The signal indicates whether a train can enter the next block. The bar projecting out from the mast held a metal banner (or lantern) to indicate train orders.

Fig. 7-13: Track warrants are much like pre-written train order forms. Train crews (not operators) receive instructions by radio and simply fill in the blanks and check the boxes, an ideal system for a model railroad.

also request that the dispatcher take CTC-controlled switches "off motor" so they can control them manually, which sets all signals protecting those switches to red.

Some railroads saved money by not powering the switches. The dispatcher simply illuminated a letter "S" to give a train crew the authority to operate the switch manually to take or leave the siding. This could also simplify model railroad wiring, as switch motors are not required.

On a model railroad, such a system offers extreme realism, especially for the dispatcher. For all practical purposes, his or her job is exactly like that of the dispatcher on a full-size railroad. The downside is the cost and complexity of designing, building, installing, and maintaining a CTC machine. Moreover, it can literally make things too easy for train crews, who simply wait for a red "traffic light" to change to green or yellow

before proceeding in a "Simon says" manner.

Manual block: An early form of train movement authority is manual block control. The main line is divided into blocks with an operator stationed at the boundary of each block. Each block station is equipped with a signal that can be set at red, yellow, or green, just like a train-order signal (fig. 7-12). Red means stop, yellow (permissive) means the block is occupied, so proceed prepared to stop short of train or obstruction, and green (clear) means proceed.

If a train order or message was waiting for an approaching crew, a red or yellow metal banner or lantern was hung from a rung on the block signal mast.

On some roads, the signal had to be left in the red position until an approaching train acknowledged its indication with a whistle blast. The operator could then clear the signal if he or she

knew, from telegraph or telephone conversations with the operator in the next block, that the block was clear. This is similar to systems in England and the eastern U.S. with towers positioned at regular intervals along the main, and operators communicated with bells or telegraph as to block availability. It translates well to model railroads where there are a lot of operators available, such as in a large club.

Track warrants: The advent of reliable two-way radio systems and changes to labor agreements allowed dispatchers to communicate directly to train crews without going through operators. To avoid mistakes, track warrant forms with blanks to fill in and boxes to check are provided. Prototype forms have around 17 lines, but a simplified 9-line form like the one Jim Providenza described in the May 1996 *Model Railroader* (fig. 7-13) will cover most modeling needs. Line 9, "other instruc-

tions," can handle a host of possibilities.

The dispatcher tells the crew to check one or more boxes and to fill in the blank in each checked line, then how many boxes they should have checked in total. The crew reads back the order, just as operators once did, to confirm the wording and number of boxes checked. The use of place names for clearance limits makes a track warrant very easy to understand. This system is almost ideal for model railroads, thanks to the availability of inexpensive multichannel radios.

Radios are somewhat anachronistic for the steam era, but they can be used as a pseudo telephone system by

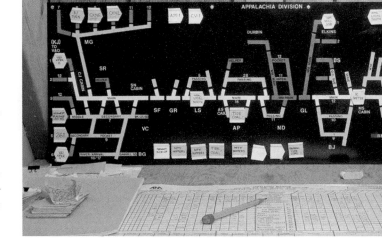

Fig. 7-14: A sheet of 24-gauge steel was used before the Allegheny Midland had a CTC machine. Magnetic markers were moved along as trains were OSed by radio or to show the clearance limits given to each train. A train sheet was used to log train movements.

Fig. 7-15: This page from a Wabash employee timetable shows the basic format, although specifics vary between railroads. It's relatively easy to mimic this format using personal-computer software. Trains 71, 13, 12, and 70 don't vanish or materialize at Wanick Jct.; they operate over another part of the Wabash beyond this point.

Direction and class of train

Location

3					TOLEDO—MONTPELIER—1st District								
Westward Trains					**Time-Table No. 40**			**Eastward Trains**					
THIRD CLASS			FIRST CLASS	Distance from Toledo		Capacity of sidings in 63 ft. cars exclusive of engine and caboose.	Station numbers	FIRST CLASS	THIRD CLASS				
79	**77**	**71**	**13**		In effect Feb. 26, 1950			**12**	**76**	**70**	**78**		
Red Ball Freight	Red Ball Freight	Local Freight	St. Louis Freight					Toledo Limited	Red Ball Freight	Local Freight	Red Ball Freight		
Daily	Daily	Daily Except Sun.	Daily		STATIONS			Daily	Daily	Daily Except Sun.	Daily		
PM	AM	AM	PM					AM	AM	PM	PM		
.....	.....	.....	6.55	.....	DN TOLEDO		1	6.50	.....	.....	.....		No. 182 depart Toledo 7:30 a.m.; arrive Oakwood Jct. 11:45 a.m. (O.S.T.).
					2.3								
9.30	10.00	7.15	6.59	1.3	23 TOLEDO Y'D WC		2	6.39	7.30	1.00	8.30		
					2.6								
9.40	10.10	7.20	7.03	3.3	WALBRIDGE JCT.	C		6.35	7.25	12.45	8.06		No. 189 depart Oakwood Jct. 2:30 a.m.; (O.S.T.) arrive Toledo 6:30 a.m.
					2.8	T							
.....	.....	.....	5.3	DN GOULD		C	5	.....	.....	.....	.....		
					3.3								Nos. 70 and 71 carry passengers.
9.50	10.20	7.40	7.10	8.6	WANICK JCT.			6.28	7.02	12.35	7.56		
					3.6								Movement of trains on Wabaab-Nickol Plate Joint Tracks Nos. 1 and 2, between Wanick Jct. and Walbridge Jct., is governed by Centralized Traffic Control and will be operated in accordance with the printed rules in Form 1764 and special instructions.
9.55	10.25	AM	PM	9.2	MAUMEE		9	AM	7.00	PM	7.53		
					3.4								
10.05	10.35	.....	.....	12.6	MONCLOVA		332	.....	6.40	.....	7.41		
					4.6								
10.17	10.47	.....	.....	17.2	MIDWAY	99	333	.....	6.25	.....	7.26		
					5.9								
10.32	11.02	.....	.....	22.2	BRAILEY		334	.....	6.10	.....	7.11		
					4.1								
10.47	11.17	.....	.....	26.3	DELTA		336	.....	5.57	.....	6.59		
					3.1								
10.55	11.25	.....	.....	29.4	DELTA YARD	112	337	.....	5.47	.....	6.49		
					4.3								
11.55	11.45	.....	.....	33.7	D WAUSEON F	66	338	.....	5.35	.....	6.37		
					5.7								
11.30	12.00	.....	.....	39.4	ECKLEY		340	.....	5.20	.....	6.22		
					3.1								
11.40	12.10	.....	.....	42.5	ELMIRA	103	342	.....	5.10	.....	6.13		
					6.6								
12.00	12.30	.....	.....	49.1	WEST UNITY	52	344	.....	4.55	.....	5.52		
					9.2								
12.45 AM	1.15 PM	.....	.....	58.3	DN MONTPELIER WC		912	.....	4.30 AM	.....	5.30 PM		
Daily	Daily	Daily Except Sun.	Daily					Daily	Daily	Daily Except Sun.	Daily		
3:15 17.5	3:15 17.5	0:25 17.5	0:15 34.4	.....	Scheduled time / Average miles per hour			0:22 23.4	3:00 19.0	0:22 17.5	3:00 19.0		

Time and average speeds — Frequency of operation — Milepost numbers — ABS—Automatic Block Signals — Hour code (D=day, DN=day-night, 25=second shift — Stations and distance between them — Facility codes — CTC—Centralized traffic control — Siding size data — Station accounting codes

Special information

---

having a radio headset mounted at open train-order stations. Crews are out of the communication loop until they are summoned, by light, buzzer, or signal, to pick up the radio at a specific place, just as with a telephone system.

Direct Traffic Management: Since an error in the operation of a model train is not a life-threatening event (unless the resulting crash puts someone's brass engine on the floor), less fail-safe systems can be used to move trains. One of the simplest is to make a schematic diagram of the layout, including staging tracks and passing sidings. The dispatcher can then slide magnetic markers along the schematic to the limit of where he or she has cleared a train (fig. 7-14). Some smaller full-size railroads use very similar systems.

Timetable and train-order operation: We now

come to one of the oldest methods of traffic control. In a basic form, it's as simple as track warrants, or you can choose to become a student of timetable and train-order operation and explore its myriad nuances.

The first train order dates back to 1851 when Charles Minot, a superintendent on

the Erie RR, was sidetracked with a freight he was riding. After waiting several hours for an opposing train, he grew impatient and walked to a nearby commercial telegraph office. He had the operator contact the Erie agent at Goshen, N.Y., 15 miles to the west, to see if a superior train had arrived. It

hadn't, so he had the telegrapher transit this message: "HOLD EASTBOUND TRAIN UNTIL FURTHER NOTICE."

He then gave handwritten orders over his signature to the conductor and engineer of the train he was riding to "run to Goshen regardless of opposing train." The engineer refused to go, legend has

Fig. 7-16 (above left): Monon Form 19 order 223, issued Sept. 30, 1967, is a standard Form G run-extra order with an important addition: Extra 517 South can't head to the Shops at Lafayette, Ind., until Extra 501 North arrives at Haskells. Had Extra 517 South been created without the "after" clause, a "lap" would have been created, as no meeting point was specified between the two extras.

Fig. 7-17 (above): Nickel Plate Form 31 order 9 issued June 8, 1964, established a meet between fast freights 95 and 96 at Davis, Ind., which was in manual block territory. The "Both trains occupy block" addition was required by Indiana law.

Fig. 7-18 (left): This Monon Clearance Form A accompanied order 223 (fig. 7-16) and informed the crew of Extra 517 South that two orders, 223 and 224, should be attached, but there are no messages. This serves as a check to be sure the operator didn't forget to give them a train order, and that he gave them the right orders.

it, so Minot took the throttle himself. He then repeated those orders between successive pairs of towns and arrived in Port Jervis, N.Y., several hours earlier than would have been possible by adhering to timetable schedules. Trains orders were born.

The growing popularity of timetable and train-order operation seems to be tied to the trend toward greater realism in all aspects of our modeling. Clock ratios are being slowed to allow time to do more of the work associated with full-size railroading from pumping off air brakes before leaving a yard to having the dispatcher dictate train orders to operators. In other words, we're modeling jobs, as we're discovering that the jobs themselves can be as much fun to "model" as the trains and their environment. Among the jobs that are immediately enhanced by timetable and train-order operation are those of the train crews, as most train-

movement decisions are moved onto their plate—a marked contrast to a CTC system environment.

Railroads published timetables to inform the public about passenger-train schedules, just as Amtrak and commuter lines do today, but such publicly distributed documents have no official status. To govern train movements, railroads published employee timetables, which are at the very heart of the safe and efficient operation of a railroad that operates by timetable and train-order rules.

The timetable provides the authority for the movement of regular trains subject to the rules and special instructions. It specifies the

Fig. 7-19: Train orders were delivered to both ends of a train via a hoop- or Y-shaped stick, either mounted in a stand (left) or held by a brave operator. Train crews communicated with operators and the dispatcher by tossing off messages (above). Model photo by Don Cassler

for meets at the blind siding (where no operator was stationed at either end in manual block territory) at Wingate, Ind. Other roads used 31s for orders that restricted the rights of a superior train—when the dispatcher had to know that an order was effective to the superior train before he or she could authorize the use of the order by an inferior train.

Both the engineer and conductor of the train receiving a 31 usually have to sign for it to be sure everyone understands the change. The operator sets the train-order signal to red to stop the train so the Form 31 can be signed for.

Don't confuse the types of orders—Forms 19 and 31—with the alpha codes that specify the standardized ways to word orders: forms A, C, D, E, and so on. Form 19s are typically 6¾" to 7" wide by 6" to 7½" high printed on very thin light green paper; 31s are the same width and up to 9" high (to provide space for the signatures) on light yellow paper, although both colors and dimensions varied among railroads. The thin paper, hence the nickname "flimsies," allowed crews to read them by holding them up to the dim light of a lantern or open firebox door.

The process of issuing a train order is initiated when the dispatcher calls an open station and says, for example, "Cayuga, 19 [or 31] west, copy three." The Cayuga operator sets the westbound train-order signal to the proper indication and says, "Signal displayed west." The operator always has enough sheets of carbon paper inserted in manifolds of train order sheets to make almost any required number of copies—here, one for his file and one each for the conduc-

it an extra train. Meeting points are often shown in bold-face type (or underscored), often with the numbers of the trains meeting there in small type.

Extra trains—those not listed in the timetable—are created when the dispatcher issues a Form G train order [see Appendix section A-3]: "Eng 517 run extra A to F" (fig. 7-16). Orders creating extras and handling other routine movements are typically issued as Form 19s, which crews can pick up on the fly as they pass an open train-order station. The train-order signal is set to green to signify no orders or messages are to be picked up or to yellow for messages or Form 19 orders.

The use of Form 31 orders (fig. 7-17) was not consistent among railroads, and some didn't use them at all. A dispatcher who handled the part of the NKP I'm modeling said he used Form 31s only

schedule of all trains (fig. 7-15) and defines superiority by class (first, second, third, and occasionally fourth) and direction (trains headed east and north usually being superior to those going west or south).

Timetable schedules are in

effect for 12 hours, which means a train can operate up to 12 hours late without losing its authority. After the 12 hours are up, the late train loses its authority and schedule and can't move an inch unless the dispatcher issues a train order to make tor and engineer of the affected train. If two or more stations must copy the same order, the dispatcher addresses it first to the station at which a superior train will receive the order.

The measured cadence of dictating the train order then begins, a sound that is as much a part of the magic of railroading as the steam whistle or diesel exhaust. The dispatcher assigns the order a number, with order 1 being the first one issued after 12:01 a.m. each day. He spells all numerals and proper names as he writes the order in a master book as it is being dictated to one or more operators. The operator(s) repeats it to the dispatcher to ensure accuracy before handing it to all affected trains, and the dispatcher underlines every word during each read-back as a cross-check.

After he or she has checked the order, the dispatcher tells the operator(s) to make it "complete" at that time. "Complete" means that the order is correct and may be delivered to the proper train(s) when it arrives. Only completed orders may be acted upon, and the same order must be issued to all affected trains. Orders are in effect until they are fulfilled, superseded, or annulled. Orders are superseded by using the words "instead of," as in "No 10 meet Extra 707 West at Linden instead of Cayuga". Note that the number "zero" is spoken and spelled "naught," as in 707: seven-naught-seven. (No. "10" is referred to as "ten," not "one-naught.")

Before the train(s) specified in each order arrives, the operator calls the dispatcher to ask him whether he has anything else for train no. 10, for example. If the dispatcher replies, "Nothing more for

no. 10," the operator fills out a clearance card and reads it to the dispatcher (fig. 7-18). Then, along with any orders, he "hoops it up" (delivers it on a hoop- or Y-shaped stick) to the train (fig. 7-19).

After the train departs, the operator calls the dispatcher to announce, "OS Cayuga." When the dispatcher responds, the operator says, "No. 10 by at 10:35 p.m. (or just "35," as everyone is keenly aware what the hour is). The dispatcher writes that time on his sprawling train sheet (fig. 7-20) in the column he has denoted for that train and in the row for that town.

Not all operator stations are open 24 hours a day, denoted as "DN" (for day and night) in the timetable. Dispatchers must keep this in mind as they decide where to issue train orders. Some stations are open only during the daytime trick at times specifically given in the timetable.

The basics of timetable and train-order operation aren't hard to learn. If you're an eastbound first-class passenger train (or, on a few roads, a first-class freight), you own the railroad—barring train orders to the contrary. A westbound first-class train without orders need watch out only for eastbound varnish. Second-class eastbound freights need be concerned only with first-class trains, but second-class westbounds are inferior to first- and second-class eastbounds. A lowly extra freight has to look out for everyone, according to when the timetable says they're due (and 12 hours thereafter if they're late, unless a helpful train order is issued), but to-move-or-not-to-move decisions are made by the local's crew, not the dispatcher, unless a new order is issued.

It takes time to dictate and copy, then repeat, a train order, and crews need to become reasonably proficient in reading timetables and working with train orders. But timetable and train-order operation provides a tremendous bonus on a model railroad: It tends to keep train crews focused, as they truly have some "skin in the game."

By using relatively slow clock ratios (3:1, 2:1, or even 1:1), operators have time to copy and crews have time to digest train orders and timetable schedules, so a pressure-cooker environment is avoided. But you can't have a timetable without a way of measuring time, so finding the proper clock ratio, usually through some trial and error during early operating sessions, is worthy of considerable contemplation.

Setting up a timetable will take some thought and

Fig. 7-20: A primary requirement for a dispatcher's office in train-order territory was a large desk for the huge train sheet. The standard clock kept everything in sync on this portion of the Southern Pacific in the 1950s. Philip R. Hastings photo

effort. You'll need to establish numbers and departure times for all of the scheduled trains you plan to run. Which stations are open when must be established. This is where prototype modelers have an edge, as an employee timetable for the era they're modeling will provide those times for a key location. The entire schedule probably won't work, as the distances are greatly shortened on the model, so one key location such as a major yard will need to be selected as a time reference point.

The timetable also contains special instructions.

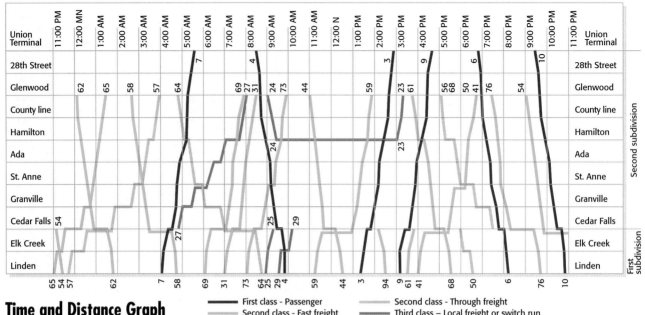

Time and Distance Graph

Legend:
- First class – Passenger
- Second class – Fast freight
- Second class – Through freight
- Third class – Local freight or switch run

Fig. 7-21: A time and distance graph is where timetable preparation starts. Bill Darnaby created this graph by starting with the Maumee's most important trains: eastbound manifests. Delays to inferior trains at meeting points are noted by horizontal breaks in the slope of the line—time continues but distance traveled is zero. The slope of the line signifies speed, which can be estimated (make triangle-shaped cardstock templates with slopes matching typical train speeds such as 30, 45, and 60 mph) or based on test runs over the layout. Bill used this graph to prepare a timetable.

This very important section includes a statement as to which direction is superior, modifications and additions to rules, train register locations, where various types of signaling (manual block, ABS, CTC, etc.) are in effect, yard instructions, locomotive weight restrictions, helper instructions, special whistle signals at interlockings, changes to rules, lists of weight restrictions, tonnage ratings, special

signal indications, location and type of interlocking plants, and speed restrictions, among other items. If there's something your crews will need to know on an ongoing basis, as opposed to just for a few days or weeks, put it in the special instructions. Train orders can handle short-lived concerns such as a speed restriction due to bad track.

The train schedules shown in a timetable can be created using a time and distance ("string-line") graph (fig. 7-21). Such graphs may appear intimidating, but they're very simple to construct. Once you work with one of these graphs for a while, you'll be able to tell at a glance which way a train is headed (time always marches to the right) and where it stops to work or for a meet or pass, as the line is flat there—that is, time continues but distance does not change. Bill Darnaby thoroughly described the entire timetable preparation process on pages 80–87 of January 1993 *Model Railroader*.

Finding a set of train schedules that actually work for your railroad takes some

time, so Walt Schumann used spreadsheet software, which allows schedules to be easily and quickly revised and redrawn (fig. 7-22). Walt explained the process on pages 112-113 of the June 1995 MR.

Where do you start? Begin with the most important trains on your schedule, which may not be first-class trains. Bill started with his fast freights, as they would set the tone for his operating sessions. Since his railroad is freelanced, he based Maumee schedules on those of similar prototype railroads in his region such as the Nickel Plate and Wabash.

From a completed time and distance graph, an employee timetable can be prepared (fig. 7-15). Study this example closely, as it shows the way most employee timetables are laid out: station names in the center, siding capacity to the right, hours of operation to the left (you can't issue a train order at a station that is closed!), trains running in the superior direction to the right, and so on. Note that trains are grouped by classes but within them listed in

order of departure starting at midnight.

Dispatchers issue train orders according to standardized forms, but they still have a lot of latitude. You can, for example, hold a superior train by ordering it to "wait at" a given point for another train, usually until a specific time has come and gone, or you could simply give the inferior train "right over" the superior train to the point in question.

The most common type of order is a meet order: "No 9 meet no 10 at Cayuga". Note the lack of punctuation, which is seldom used in train orders. Another common order creates an extra train: "Eng 639 run extra Frankfort to Charleston". (See Appendix section A-3.)

What you want to avoid is a "lap" order, which simply means you have given overlapping authority to two trains. If you had created Extra 639 West with the preceding order, you couldn't then issue this order: "Eng 707 run extra Charleston to Frankfort"—there is no meeting point specified between these two extras— unless you added something

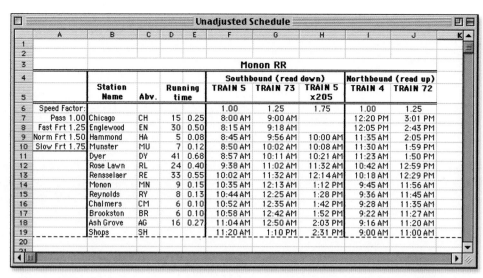

Fig. 7-22: Walt Shumann used spreadsheet software to log train schedules (right), then had the data plotted to show meeting points. When they occurred between passing tracks, he adjusted departure times to move the meet to a logical place (below). One or both trains' speeds could also be tweaked. Making such adjustments on a PC is much easier than doing calculations and plots manually.

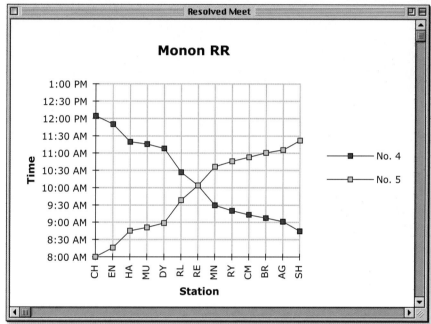

like "take siding and meet Extra 639 West at Cayuga".

Regular trains need not know of the existence of either extra, as they are not specified in the meet order. It's up to the crews of the extras to move between stations or even occupy the main track only during periods shown in the timetable to be free of scheduled trains (and 12 hours thereafter if they are late).

How do the trains know when a scheduled train has arrived? Register books are located at originating terminals, branch junctions, and other key points, and all trains must register there for just that reason.

If you break down on the main line, you must immediately send out a flagman to protect both ends of your train on single track, and the rear end on double track, per Rule 99 (see Appendix, section A-2). You can go anywhere by flagging, although this doesn't condone needlessly delaying superior trains.

Those interested in a thorough review of how railroads moved traffic should read the book *Rights of Trains*, which was updated by Peter Josserand (Simmons-Boardman), recently reprinted in softcover format.

Procedures directories

Even a professional railroader can't remember every detail he or she will ever need to know about train procedures, such as the blocking of and work performed by every train on the system. Railroads large and small therefore benefit from a train procedures manual that describes each train's consist by block and the work it does along the line.

This information is helpful to yardmasters, who direct the makeup of each train, as well as to the crews that operate them. A condensed version of each train's work description makes an excellent cover sheet for each packet of waybills handed to outbound crews. Doug Gurin and Allen McClelland discussed the Virginian & Ohio's train procedures directory on pages 75–80 of the January 1979 issue of *Railroad Model Craftsman;* that article was reprinted in *The V&O Story*, a softcover book by McClelland (Carstens Publications). Bill

Gruber described a similar procedures manual used on his Reading RR layout on pages 72–75 of the January 1992 *Railroad Model Craftsman.*

CHAPTER EIGHT

Signal systems

Fig. 8-1: The eastbound signal on the right shows yellow-over-red—"approach"—as two sets of C&O Geeps work Quinnimont, W. Va., in April 1973. The standard rectangular tower (QN Cabin in C&O parlance) atop the yardmaster's office was closed when CTC was installed. The C&O made extensive use of cantilever signal bridges.

Signals serve a dual purpose on prototype railroads: They help to manage the movement of trains, and they enhance safety (fig. 8-1). Model railroaders have discovered a third benefit: They look cool (fig. 8-2).

Each signal has an aspect, a name, and an indication. The aspect is the appearance—the color, or the position of the blade or row of lights—of a signal. Its name is the word you use when talking about it, such as "clear," "approach," or "stop." The indication is what the signal tells you to do, such as "proceed," "proceed prepared to stop at next signal at or below medium speed," or "stop." Fig. 8-3 shows typical aspects, names, and indications for a variety of signal types.

Fig. 8-2: The B&O used both color and position aspects to convey signal indications. This involves a lot of wiring, but the result is both an operational and visual treat on Don Cassler's spectacular HO railroad. Don Cassler photo

Fig. 8-3 (below): This chart shows typical signal aspect (color), name, and indication with the associated rule.

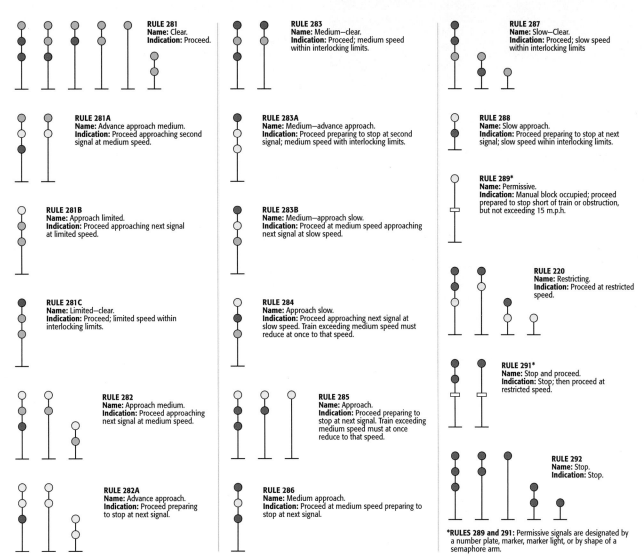

RULE 281
Name: Clear.
Indication: Proceed.

RULE 281A
Name: Advance approach medium.
Indication: Proceed approaching second signal at medium speed.

RULE 281B
Name: Approach limited.
Indication: Proceed approaching next signal at limited speed.

RULE 281C
Name: Limited–clear.
Indication: Proceed; limited speed within interlocking limits.

RULE 282
Name: Approach medium.
Indication: Proceed approaching next signal at medium speed.

RULE 282A
Name: Advance approach.
Indication: Proceed preparing to stop at next signal.

RULE 283
Name: Medium–clear.
Indication: Proceed; medium speed within interlocking limits.

RULE 283A
Name: Medium–advance approach.
Indication: Proceed preparing to stop at second signal; medium speed with interlocking limits.

RULE 283B
Name: Medium–approach slow.
Indication: Proceed at medium speed approaching next signal at slow speed.

RULE 284
Name: Approach slow.
Indication: Proceed approaching next signal at slow speed. Train exceeding medium speed must reduce at once to that speed.

RULE 285
Name: Approach.
Indication: Proceed preparing to stop at next signal. Train exceeding medium speed must at once reduce to that speed.

RULE 286
Name: Medium approach.
Indication: Proceed at medium speed preparing to stop at next signal.

RULE 287
Name: Slow–Clear.
Indication: Proceed; slow speed within interlocking limits

RULE 288
Name: Slow approach.
Indication: Proceed preparing to stop at next signal; slow speed within interlocking limits.

RULE 289*
Name: Permissive.
Indication: Manual block occupied; proceed prepared to stop short of train or obstruction, but not exceeding 15 m.p.h.

RULE 220
Name: Restricting.
Indication: Proceed at restricted speed.

RULE 291*
Name: Stop and proceed.
Indication: Stop; then proceed at restricted speed.

RULE 292
Name: Stop.
Indication: Stop.

***RULES 289 and 291:** Permissive signals are designated by a number plate, marker, marker light, or by shape of a semaphore arm.

Standard Hand Signals

1. GO FORWARD
USE: In switching.
Flat hand moved up and down about wrist. Speed or size of motion controls speed of train.

2. GO BACKWARD
USE: In switching.
Hand with pointing finger moved in circle. Speed or size of circular motion controls speed of train.

3. STOP
USE: For general stopping. Flat hands are waved across each other or hand is dropped.

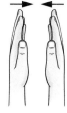

4. CONTROLLED STOP
USE: For coupling or uncoupling. Hands brought together at a speed so as to touch at a desired stopping place. Distance between hands equals the distance between cars to be coupled on model coupler pair to uncoupling ramp distance.

5. INCHING
USE: To take up slack or to move short distances. Combination of 1 or 2 with one hand while other uses fingers like 4 for distance.

6. THROW TURNOUT
USE: In switching only to request tower operator to throw turnout. Tap top of head with one hand and point to desired track for which turnout is to be aligned with the other.

7. HIGHBALL
USE: All switching complete and/or train cleared to proceed. Thumb and forefinger form a circle (Like "all okay")

Fig. 8-4 (left): Photo Electric of Salem, Ore., custom-built this CTC machine for the Allegheny Midland. It follows standard Union Switch & Signal practices. The wiring was planned around Bruce Chubb's Computer/Model Railroad Interface software and detectors. Much of the hardware was from actual US&S machines.

Fig. 8-5 (above): Hand signals used by professional railroaders can be seen at considerable distances. Model railroad hand signals have been adapted to the close quarters around a model railroad, where swinging a lantern about is considered inappropriate.

The ultimate application of signaling to a model railroad is through a Centralized Traffic Control (CTC) system, as we reviewed in Chapter 7 on moving trains. The dedicated modeler who is willing to do a lot of homework and spend a significant number of hobby dollars on the design and construction of the CTC machine, signals, and detectors can be rewarded with hardware of incredible realism (fig. 8-4). In fact, since actual CTC machine parts are often used or replicated, there is little actual "modeling" involved where the machine and dispatcher's office are concerned.

There are far less costly and complex ways to enjoy the use of signals on a model railroad, however, as we'll explore in the following pages. And no matter how deeply you decide to delve into signaling, most of the hardware and software you'll need to install the system of your choice is commercially available.

Hand and whistle signals

Signaling also embraces the use of hand and whistle or horn signals to communicate to others. In the narrow confines of the railroad room most modelers use their index fingers or hands rather than their entire arms to make the appropriate motions (fig. 8-5).

Whistle signals have assumed more importance during operating sessions with the advent of onboard sound systems. Most of us already know the two longs, a short, and a long signal that an engineer blows when approaching a road grade crossing, but we're a little rusty when it comes to sending out a flag or calling attention to the green flags we're carrying. The accompa-

nying chart (fig. 8-6) should get you up to speed.

Don't feel self-conscious about using hand and whistle signals, and proper terminology, as you operate your railroad. The whole idea is to replicate the actions of a full-size railroad and the railroaders who run it, and signals of all types are an important, even colorful, part of railroading.

Train-order signals

In timetable and train-order territory, train crews had to know whether an operator had train orders or messages for them to pick up. They were alerted by some form of train-order signal (fig. 8-7).

Train-order signals typically displayed green for no orders or messages, yellow for a Form 19 order or message, and red for a Form 31 order. The latter, if used at all, required the conductor

and engineer to sign for it before the dispatcher could make it "complete."

Manual block signals

Manual blocks were discussed in Chapter 7. These served the same function as automatic blocks but with human operators instead of automatic track circuitry: They ensured that not more than one train occupied a block unless special provisions were made.

Rule 317 states that a train may not enter a block known to be occupied by an opposing train or a passenger train unless so authorized by a train order. Operators blocked following freights at least five minutes apart except when visibility was poor; 15-minute intervals were then used. When a block station is closed, all lights must be extinguished and the signals positioned to indicate "proceed."

Whistle and Horn Signals

Fig. 8-6:
A short sound is designated by "o" and a long sound by "–"

o	Apply brakes. Stop.
– –	Release brakes. Proceed.
– o o o	Flagman protect rear of train.
– – – –	Flagman may return from west or south.
– – – – –	Flagman may return from east or north.
o o	Answer to any signal not otherwise provided for.
o o o	When standing, back. When running, stop at next station.
o o o o	Call for signals.
– o o	Call attention to signals displayed for a following section.
– – o –	Road crossing, with last long extended until train occupies crossing.
–	Approaching stations, junctions, and railroad crossings [extend the long].
– – o	Approaching meeting or waiting point.
o –	Inspect train for sticking brake.
Repeated o	Alarm for persons or livestock on track.

There are also other signals for use in special situations, such as recalling a flagman on a multi-track main line.

Here's how two operators could move a train through a block: The operator at Town A would check the block records to be sure the block was clear and then call the operator at Town B and say, "Display stop signal for No. 10." Town B would reply, "Block clear for No. 10," or words to that effect. The train's entry into and departure from the block is duly reported by the appropriate operator to each other and to the dispatcher.

Some railroads required that the train crew whistle for, then actually see the manual block signal being cleared. This kept a train from running into an occupied block when an operator had forgotten to change the signal indication from "clear" back to "stop."

Indiana had a law requiring that Form 31 orders be used to allow two trains into the same manual block, as

Fig. 8-7: Three of the many types of train-order signals are shown here: upper-quadrant semaphore on the NKP at Montmorenci, Ind. (top), searchlight at G Office on the NKP and NYC in Lafayette, Ind. (center), and a lower-quadrant semaphore at Duncan, N.C., on the old Norfolk Southern (bottom).

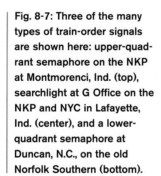

for a meet when the train crew controlled the siding entrance switch. The 31 order had to state "Both trains occupy block." If one of the meeting trains headed into a siding at a switch controlled by an operator, however, that train was not considered to be in the next block, so a Form 19 order could be used.

Manual block signals were occasionally used on double-tracked railroads where ABS was also used in one direction on each track. Trains running on the "wrong main"

could then be protected by manual block signals.

One caveat: Implementing a full-blown manual block system on a model railroad might take some of the train-movement initiative away from train crews. It might work well on a large club layout, where the extra personnel are available and the extra train-movement help is needed, but it could negate a lot of the challenge and enjoyment that accrues from

a single-track main line run under timetable and train-order authority.

Automatic block signals

Like manual block signals, automatic block signals (fig. 8-8) govern the use of blocks but, unlike CTC signals, do not supersede the superiority of trains except in multitrack territory so specified by the timetable. Trains approaching a stop signal must stop clear of that

Block Signals

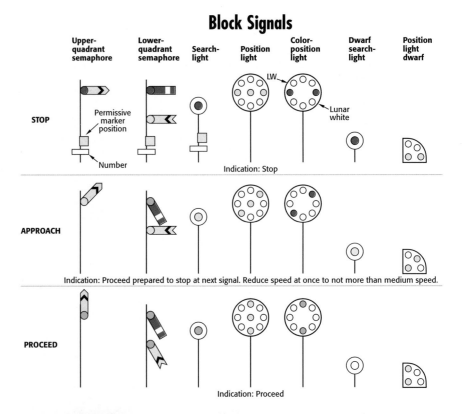

	Upper-quadrant semaphore	Lower-quadrant semaphore	Search-light	Position light	Color-position light	Dwarf search-light	Position light dwarf
STOP	Permissive marker position / Number				LW / Lunar white		

Indication: Stop

| **APPROACH** | | | | | | | |

Indication: Proceed prepared to stop at next signal. Reduce speed at once to not more than medium speed.

| **PROCEED** | | | | | | | |

Indication: Proceed

Fig. 8-9: What's this—a green home signal (above) at Davis Jct., Ill., in 1979 as a Milwaukee Road freight works on the Burlington Northern main? Nope: The view looking the other direction (above right) shows the home signal in the distance; the green signal indicates there are no train orders or messages to pick up. Lloyd Rinehart photos

signal. If the signal mast has a number plate, indicating stop-and-proceed, the train

may proceed at restricted speed after coming to a stop. Heavy freights approaching a "grade" signal, denoted by a yellow disk, a plate with a letter "G," or as otherwise provided may pass the signal at restricted speed without stopping.

Once a train or locomotive has left a block, it may not back into that block except by flagging (rule 99). The same applies to a train backing or being pulled out of a siding onto the main line.

Absolute-Permissive Block signals

Single-track main lines often use Absolute-Permissive Block, or APB, signaling. APB is a form of ABS that has an added safety feature to prevent opposing trains from coming head-to-head between a pair of sidings. The name comes from absolute (stop) "head-block" signals at the entrance to a stretch of single-track main between two passing tracks, plus permissive (stop, then proceed at restricted speed) signals

between the two absolutes.

When a train passes the absolute signal at the end of a siding, APB then drops all signals for opposing trains between there and the next siding to red. As the train moves toward the next siding, signals behind it gradually clear to permit trailing movements, as with regular ABS.

Jay Boggess wrote an extensive series of articles on APB beginning in the November 1991 *Model Railroader*. Rich Weyand

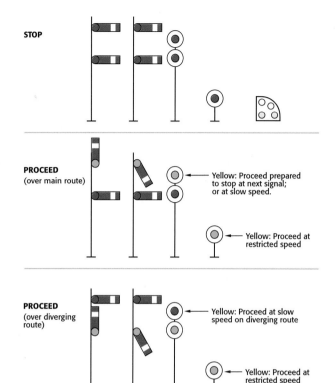

Interlocking Signals

STOP

PROCEED (over main route)

Yellow: Proceed prepared to stop at next signal; or at slow speed.

Yellow: Proceed at restricted speed

PROCEED (over diverging route)

Yellow: Proceed at slow speed on diverging route

Yellow: Proceed at restricted speed

Interlocking Distant Signals

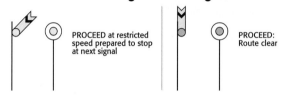

PROCEED at restricted speed prepared to stop at next signal

PROCEED: Route clear

Fig. 8-10: Lafayette Jct., Ind. (top), was where the joint NKP-NYC double-track main crossed the Monon and Wabash. This westbound NKP (N&W) local has just crossed over the Wabash (also N&W) in May 1967 and is passing under the signal bridge that supports Monon (at left) and Wabash home signals.

covered APB circuitry in the November 1994 *Mainline Modeler.*

Interlocking signals

The term "interlock" refers to mechanical and electrical devices that prevent an operator from setting up conflicting routes through interlocking limits (figs. 8-9 and 8-10). Once a route through the plant is established, either by a towerman or an automatic circuit, it can't be taken away without running a timer. This ensures that a rapidly approaching train won't suddenly see a green signal change to red.

Interlocking signals govern the use of the routes through an interlocking plant and, like CTC, their indications supersede the superiority of trains as to movements within home-signal limits. The home interlocking signal may also be used as a block signal.

It would be unsafe to have a heavy train approach an interlocking plant at speed, only to find a red home signal. In most cases, a distant signal is therefore located sufficiently in advance of the home signal to convey a yellow warning aspect if the home signal is red.

CTC signals

Centralized Traffic Control (CTC) dates back to a General Railway Signal Co. (GRS) installation on the New York Central from Stanley to Berwick, O., in 1927. GRS and Union Switch & Signal were the major suppliers of CTC systems. Another name for CTC is a "traffic control system," which in 1950 the Interstate Commerce Commission defined as "a block system under which train movements are authorized by block signals whose indications supersede the superiority of trains for both opposing and following movements on the same track."

CTC territory is designated by the timetable and special instructions. Signs stating "BEGIN [or END] CTC" are posted along the main line (fig. 8-11). A third-class train moves with the same rights as a first-class train—according to signal indication—although the dispatcher will obviously make every effort to keep the more important trains moving.

A CTC system is really nothing more than a succession of interlockings

Fig. 8-11: The beginning and ending of CTC territory are marked with signs such as this one on the UP's line running north from Las Vegas to Caliente. Union Switch & Signal photo

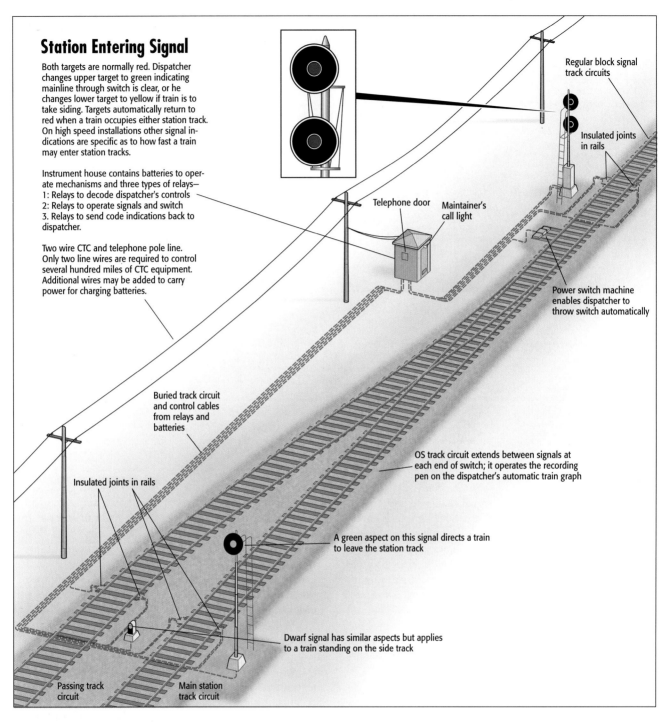

Station Entering Signal

Both targets are normally red. Dispatcher changes upper target to green indicating mainline through switch is clear, or he changes lower target to yellow if train is to take siding. Targets automatically return to red when a train occupies either station track. On high speed installations other signal indications are specific as to how fast a train may enter station tracks.

Instrument house contains batteries to operate mechanisms and three types of relays—
1: Relays to decode dispatcher's controls
2: Relays to operate signals and switch
3. Relays to send code indications back to dispatcher.

Two wire CTC and telephone pole line. Only two line wires are required to control several hundred miles of CTC equipment. Additional wires may be added to carry power for charging batteries.

Buried track circuit and control cables from relays and batteries

Insulated joints in rails

Passing track circuit

Main station track circuit

Telephone door

Maintainer's call light

Regular block signal track circuits

Insulated joints in rails

Power switch machine enables dispatcher to throw switch automatically

OS track circuit extends between signals at each end of switch; it operates the recording pen on the dispatcher's automatic train graph

A green aspect on this signal directs a train to leave the station track

Dwarf signal has similar aspects but applies to a train standing on the side track

controlled from a single machine (fig. 8-12). A schematic diagram of the railroad is shown across the top of the panel (figs. 7-11 and 8-4). Some panels also show a profile of the railroad.

Each dispatcher-controlled switch is an "OS section," a term carried over from operators reporting trains past their stations—"on sheet" or "out of station." These sections automatically report the passing of a train by illuminating a light (and sometimes ringing a bell). Signals at the points end of OS sections usually have two or three heads that display aspects such as green over red (clear—proceed), red over green (medium clear—proceed at medium speed within interlocking limits), or red over red (stop—fig. 8-13).

Between OS sections may be one or more sets of ABS signals, over which the dispatcher has no control. He may have control of a hold-out signal, however, which allows trains to be held at a specific spot.

Train crews do not need train orders to move through CTC territory, but they still need a clearance form authorizing them to be on the rail-

Fig. 8-12: A typical OS section in CTC territory is depicted by this drawing. It could be controlled by a local tower operator or a distant dispatcher.

road. Trains carrying passengers or U.S. mail may not pass or leave a place where passengers or mail is received in advance of their times as shown in the timetable.

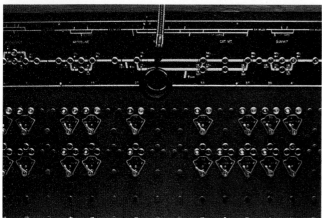

Setting up a meet between two opposing trains using a CTC panel is easy. Let's say the train approaching from the right is going into the "hole" (passing track) at Rockpoint on David Barrow's Cat Mountain & Santa Fe using switch 17 (fig. 8-14). On the top row of the panel, the dispatcher moves the lever for that switch from the "N" (normal) position to "R" (reverse).

He then moves the signal levers in the second row for all blocks to the right of the meeting point to the left to allow the train on the right to move to the left up to and into the siding at Rockpoint. He also moves the signal levers to the left side of the meeting point to the right to allow the train holding the main to move up to the reversed switch.

That done, he then hits a code-start button below each column of levers to send his commands out to the field. Until that button is pushed, moving the switch and signal levers on the panel has no effect. If this were an actual US&S machine, relays in the CTC machine would clatter "ka-chunk, ka-chunk-a-chunk-a-chunk" as the coded commands pulsed out over communication lines to relays at Rockpoint. There the code would be converted into electrical signals causing the switch motor to reverse the points.

The signals then indicate to the train from the right that it will head in to the siding, and to the opposing train that it must stop clear of the switch. On the prototype, the movement of the switchpoints and the signal indications are confirmed with coded messages sent back to the CTC machine and displayed on the panel.

As soon as the train from the right has entered the OS section, as indicated by a red light on the panel, the dispatcher may move the switch lever back to "N" (normal) and the associated signal levers from left to right for the impending move to the right. Even if he then hits the code button to "precondition" the machine, nothing will happen in the field because the machine has that route locked up until the train entering the siding has cleared that OS section. When the train is tucked safely into the siding, the switchpoints will automatically move, and signal 18R will clear for the train that held the main.

A route out of the siding is just as easily set up and activated when the train occupying the main has cleared the switch 15's OS section. The dispatcher puts switch lever 15 to "R" (reverse) and moves the signal toggles to the left to indicate a move in that direction. Signal 16L will then clear up after the points have moved to the reversed position.

You'll therefore want to buy or photocopy a rule book and employee timetable for the railroad and period you're modeling to be sure you follow their signaling practices.

Ken Thompson described the CTC machine and circuitry used on David Barrow's CM&SF on pages 74–80 of the May 1984 *Model Railroader*.

CHAPTER NINE

The operating session

Fig. 9-1: There's plenty of room in the aisle for Don Cabrall, Morgan Trotter, and, behind Morgan, Bill Kaufman to do their jobs on Jim Providenza's Santa Cruz Northern as long as no kibitzers are hanging around. George Hall photo

Your first formal operating session is where it all comes together, like a play opening on (or off) Broadway. Expectations are high, opportunities abound, yet problems lurk at every turn. Just as actors miss their cues or forget their lines, missteps are bound to occur. What have you overlooked or incorrectly assumed? Will enough operators show up? What will derail where, and when?

Relax: It's a learning experience. No one can know everything, especially at first. The crews are as nervous as you are, as they don't want to screw up in front of their peers.

Your primary job is therefore to get everyone onto the same page. Hold a brief meeting before this and each subsequent session to go over expectations, changes since the last session, where the bathroom is located, and so on. Make everyone feel at home, and you'll be more comfortable too. They are, after all, your guests.

People management

Holding an operating session with more than a few operators is an exercise in people management. Don't underestimate the importance of this task. If you don't set expectations properly, you'll never have smooth sessions.

Selecting, or developing, and retaining good operators is the key. It's not rocket science, but they do have to get with the program. If you can't count on someone to show up regularly, find someone else who has a more flexible schedule or better appreciates what you're trying to accomplish. If they seem hesitant, get together with them individually to work through their concerns.

Most railroads operate best with a specific crew size. Too few or too many operators can spoil the session as quickly as derailments or electrical problems. Only the largest layouts can accommodate virtually anyone who walks in the door. Beyond a certain point, aisle congestion can plug up the railroad as surely as too many freight cars in a yard (fig. 9-1).

Jack Ozanich has addressed this problem in a novel way. He can't readily accommodate an unexpected number, high or low, of operators on short notice, but if he knows well in advance that several sessions in a row will be poorly attended, as in the summer months, he switches from the labor-intensive steam era to a more modern era that requires fewer operators. For example, train length can be increased by adding multiple diesel units, which allows running fewer trains, if he knows what to expect.

Other owners have developed rosters of operators who, barring some sort of unforeseen disaster, always attend their sessions or invariably give several days' notice of their pending absence. The owners can then call others from the extra board. If someone drops out permanently, someone else on the extra board is "promoted."

The most chronic people problems seem to occur when attendance and visitor etiquette is not clear. We have more fun when we don't have to worry about unexpected problems cropping up and spoiling our good time, and common courtesy contributes to that serenity.

Personality clashes may occur. If they are allowed to fester, the ill will can spread to the entire crew. As at school or work, such clashes should be dealt with promptly and firmly. Clear heads usually prevail, and as in most family squabbles, the crisis soon passes. If not, crew roster changes may be required.

Some operators have two entirely separate crews. One may operate on, say, the second Saturday afternoon of the month, the other on the fourth Friday evening. Individuals can often be moved between these two groups to minimize personality conflicts.

Visitors

Visitors are a touchy subject. Large railroads may have enough jobs to accommodate a visiting fireman or two, but many first-time visitors profess that they "just want to watch." That's not a good idea, as the already-busy host feels obligated to show them around, and crew members take time to explain what they're doing. It sounds

warm and cozy, but it usually detracts from a session if this occurs with any regularity. Moreover, they often get in the way.

Everyone needs to understand that they are not to bring visitors without the host's approval, as too many visitors jeopardize the quality of the session for the regulars. It's the regulars, after all, who need to be accommodated, or they'll melt away.

My own policy evolved to inviting a first timer to visit the railroad on a non-operating night or Saturday morning when I could devote my undivided attention to him

Fig. 9-4: Mine runs usually offer a chance to get off the busy main line and work in a secluded mountain valley. Here the Low Gap Shifter drifts downgrade past a tipple owned by Wheeling Steel as it takes loads to the main line at Big Springs Jct., W. Va.

Fig. 9-5 (left): The Midland Road's original dispatcher's office was a cubbyhole under the basement stairs equipped with a desk, radio, fast-time clock, and magnetic schematic panel. It was a simple but very effective means of controlling the railroad.

or her. Only if the visitor was a highly experienced operator who could fit right in with little or no coaching did I extend an initial invitation to a formal operating session. I tried to give first-time visitors a taste of operation by having them help me stage the railroad by moving coal loads back to tipples and passenger trains to the opposite ends of the railroad.

An interesting aside: Allen McClelland is frequently asked whether he runs trains "just for fun" between sessions. His reply, and my own to such questions, is that he does not except for staging and testing purposes. Why? Because he regards the V&O as a railroad, and railroads do things purposely. During an operating session, a moving train is Advance 95 or 261. Between sessions, it's just a model locomotive and a bunch of cars. Operation literally adds that much value to a model railroad.

Even groups of experienced operators usually can't be accommodated at regular sessions, as there aren't enough jobs for them. Teaming up with regulars may work, but a better solution may be to hold special sessions for visitors, with just enough regulars on hand to act as guides or fill key positions.

Finding operators

As I said before, an operating railroad attracts modelers. Once word gets around, you may be surprised at the inter-

est level. A notice at a local hobby shop or model railroad club or in an NMRA region or division newsletter may work wonders.

No luck? It's time to develop your own cadre of operators. Area modelers who show little interest in operation may in fact be interested but reluctant to show their ignorance. Don't ask them what they know about operation; instead, show them what you know. If they show some signs of interest or knowledge, ask for their help with a switching task or operating a train over the railroad. Have them stop it somewhere to pick up a car, and somewhere else to set out another one. Maybe have them wait at Town A for an opposing train you're operating, but be careful about leaving them on their own, as that can cause tension. Keep it light at first.

Look for types of operation that seem to interest them. They may like the mental challenge of sorting cars into blocks in a yard (fig. 9-2), or they may resist that: "Too much like work!" They may love to run a big engine and long train over the road, or they may find that soon bores them to tears (fig. 9-3). (Wait till they discover timetable and train-order operation!) They may enjoy local switching or working mines out on the road (fig.

Fig. 9-6: These two photos show the AM's Appalachia Div. crew-call board. Trains, locomotives, call points, and on-duty times were listed, and crews could mark up for one morning and one afternoon/evening job. When that job was completed, they could mark up for any open job. The use of magnets on a steel call board allowed changes to be made quickly and easily.

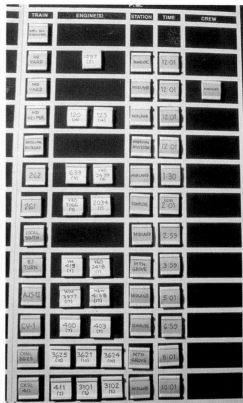

9-4)—or find it tedious. Such differences are assets, as we need a variety of interests to handle the various jobs on the railroad.

You may find that no one volunteers for some jobs. You'll either have crew members who love to be yardmasters or dispatchers (fig. 9-5) or who refuse to fill such jobs. If no one volunteers to work alongside you or someone else who can help him get his feet wet, then rotate jobs so that everyone does every job for a short while. The guy who "hated" dispatching may have to be pried out of the dispatcher's comfy chair after an hour at that job, which is usually the most realistic on the railroad.

The goal is for all jobs on the model railroad to have prototypical analogs. We want to minimize "model railroad thoughts"—having people do things that are purely model railroad functions such as dealing with reversing loops (which can be automated) or block-selector switches. Some jobs may not have analogs, however. If you want to avoid having road crews run trains in and out of hidden staging yards, for example, then you'll need to assign someone as a "staging hostler" or "Northern Division crew," where the entire Northern Division is a staging yard. This job may be combined with a "realistic

job" such as engine terminal hostler to add more content, but if no one signs up for that job, you'll have to assign it to, say, the next crew that comes off a road job. They'll do it for a while, and then another road crew will get stuck with it, and then another. They'll live.

Crew assignments

You're likely to discover that in a group of more than two or three people, there is enough variety in their primary interests to fill all key jobs. Some operators can't be pried out of the yardmaster's position; others avoid it.

The problem comes when there are a few jobs that can't easily be filled. A good way to handle this is to set a requirement that crews finishing one job must sign up for the next open job. You may want to fill key positions

Fig. 9-7: The former family room was converted to a lounge for off-duty Midland Road crews, which also kept them out of the railroad room where they could distract operators. The AM's Coal Fork Extension was located over south-end staging, which sat atop book shelves, so no additional floor space was sacrificed, and the room could still be used for family functions.

Fig. 9-9: Daylighting the south end of the AM's north-end staging yard to make it a partially visible classification yard required a new panel. The red push buttons controlled power to each track, ensuring that locomotives on trains staged on yard tracks were not receiving power until they needed to be moved.

A crew-assignment board can be nothing more than a white board with marker pens. I made one from a piece of 24-gauge sheet metal by spraying it white, applying masked tape where divided lines were desired, and then spraying a final green coat. Dry-transfer lettering was rubbed on, and the entire board was given a clear coat (fig. 9-6). Magnets used for task scheduling were cut into shorter strips, and labels for each job, locomotive, job location, and time were inserted.

I initially made two name-tag magnets for each crew member. He or she could choose one morning and one afternoon/evening job. Later, I added a third blue tag. An early arriving crew member could use his and her a.m. and p.m. markers to select any two jobs in the proper time slot, and the blue one to select a third job. Those who arrived later could not "bump" a regular marker, but they could bump a blue marker (blue for bumped). This prevented early arrivers from hogging all the good jobs while still rewarding them for being prompt.

Operating night—or day

There's no one best time to operate. I don't like to tie up weekends, so I operated on Friday nights. Others have found that a weekend day works better for them. Those who have to head off for work at 5 a.m. Saturday

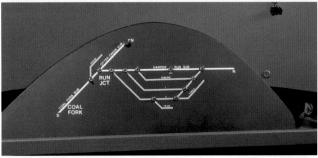

Fig. 9-8 (left): Local control panels on the Allegheny Midland's Coal Fork Extension were simple and neat. The use of command control meant that no block toggles or rotary switches cluttered up the panels. This one nestled into the curve of the fascia in one corner of the room.

Fig. 9-10: Car cards and waybills will be laid out all over the railroad if a place to store them isn't provided. Bill boxes—one for each track in all but the smallest towns—allow crew members to sort waybills as they switch cars. The green forms hanging from the fascia are trouble tickets crews could use to anonymously report problems with track, wiring, or equipment.

such as dispatcher or yardmaster with experienced operators, but encourage off-duty crew members to work with these veterans to learn the position. Nine times out of ten, their "disinterest" is really a manifestation of their lack of knowledge, which they're embarrassed to admit.

or have an early tee time on summer weekends won't want to hang around till midnight, which is when the really deep philosophical conversations about our great hobby start to blossom.

Be observant of local preferences, and be as flexible as you can. One routine won't work for everyone, but it will work for most.

Human factors

Even though we're modeling "work," we're trying to ensure that a good time is had by all. An operating session typically lasts several hours, so creature comforts are important.

For AM crews, the former family room next to the main railroad room became a crew lounge (fig. 9-7). I carpeted the railroad room inexpensively (if arduously) with used industrial carpet tiles to ease the strain on feet and knees, and the entire room was brightly illuminated with numerous fluorescent fixtures. Aging eyes, especially, need all the lumens they can get to avoid eye strain and to maintain sharp focus. And, nice as a basement bathroom would have been, AM crews could reach the upstairs bathroom without cutting through a family area.

There is no one best way to build control panels, and indeed with walk-around radio command-control throttles and manual ground throws, you may not need control panels at all. At the very least, command control has eliminated the need for block control toggles or rotary switches, and the associated panel wiring.

I made a small panel for each town on the Allegheny Midland (fig. 9-8) that sat on a ledge and was secured with kitchen cupboard magnetic catches. Town panels could be flipped over for easy access to the wiring. Yard panels were more complex (fig. 9-9), but I kept them simple and clean.

White aircraft striping tape designated the limestone-ballasted main line; yellow indicated sidings and yard tracks; green showed normally dead tracks where train or engines were stored (I don't like to leave electronics cooking needlessly); red showed where reversing sections (wyes and turntables) were located; and orange marked a foreign road. North Yard ladder switches were individually controlled, as it was a visible yard, but diode-matrix route-selection circuitry is much easier to use in hidden staging yards.

I've seen switch-point toggles or knobs mounted on the fascia directly below the switches they control, which appeals to me in that crews have to walk to the place where they're supposed to be working, not throw a switch from a scale half-mile away. Toggles should be recessed or otherwise protected, however, so passing crews won't accidentally reverse them.

Waybill boxes, one for each track, ensured that waybills could be sorted as fast as cars are switched in large towns (fig. 9-10) and at yards (fig. 4-10). A single box sufficed for small towns. The 3½"-wide shelf around the layout was handy for sorting

waybills, holding train-card packets, or setting down soft-drink containers.

Scheduling time for the railroad

I'll close with a note about the importance of a hobby. Take it from those of us who have enjoyed modeling railroading for most of our lives: It more than repays what you invest in it, no matter how that value is measured.

It follows that it's important enough to assume a place in your household budget of time and money. You know from educational and professional experiences that projects that don't have well-defined deadlines and budgets tend to get out of control or are simply ignored. They couldn't be very important or someone would have made sure they got done on time and within budget. We never would have finished those term papers if our teachers hadn't set deadlines. Publish or perish, indeed!

A hobby can't move to the head of the planning and budgeting line. That's where food and housing and transportation and education and health and even family vacations reside. But it should be a line item in your planning. It can contribute to your well-being, and that of your family, in ways you'd never expect. The social aspects alone that accrue from regular operating sessions are hard to understand until you've experienced them first hand.

Make time for your hobby. Make regular progress on the railroad. Operate it regularly.

Operating night on the Allegheny Midland

The Midland Road usually operated on the fourth Friday of each month, but this was occasionally shifted to the third Friday to avoid conflicts with major holidays. Sessions began promptly at 8:00 p.m. and lasted four hours. We used a 6:1 fast-clock ratio, which allowed us to operate an entire 24-hour day. The day was split into two 12-hour halves (two actual hours) for jobs such as dispatcher or yardmaster. I once offered to cut the sessions to three hours from four, but I got push-back: "I drive two hours to get here, so I want to railroad as long as I can!"

The railroad could run with as few as eight operators, and 12 was about the maximum it could support without people sitting around or distracting each other. Jobs ranged from a dispatcher (per 12-hour trick), two yardmasters, a crew for the shortline Ridgeley & Midland County, a Western Maryland crew, and sev-

eral local and road crews. Like many layout owners, I usually assumed the job of "Mobile One," responding to questions or fixing minor problems as the session progressed, rather than marking up for a specific job. I dispatched on occasion, and I ran trains when we were short of crews.

Road jobs included several mines runs, two branch local passenger runs (gas-electrics with trailers), two mainline way freights, and two passenger trains, plus a half-dozen through or fast freights and a number of empty or loaded coal trains. A dozen hidden staging tracks were located at each end of the railroad to support this level of activity (see "AM Staging" diagram). All staging tracks were pre-assigned to avoid conflicts between inbound and outbound trains.

The Allegheny Midland operated from day one with Dynatrol analog command-control. I later added three of Dynatrol's infrared

wireless throttles (cabs), which worked well. All AM and parent Nickel Plate Road steam locomotives were equipped with their steam sound system, which was excellent but did not include whistle or bell sounds, with two exceptions—a 2-8-4 and a 4-8-4 generously loaned to the AM by Karen Parker. In my view, the engines without sound seemed like ghosts that noiselessly drifted along the railroad, and my ongoing switch to DCC is to a large extent motivated by the availability of more steam sounds and a full complement of diesel sounds.

Four through freights and two local freights were made up or broken down at the AM's main classification yard in Sunrise, Va. Mine shifters worked out of a smaller yard at South Fork, W. Va. South Fork was originally conceived as another division-point yard but proved too small for that task, so the division point was moved into the north-end staging yard (North

The main theme of Allegheny Midland operations was the movement of coal from tipples southeast to tidewater or north toward the Great Lakes. Here the Otter Creek Shifter works Dixie Coal's two-track tipple at Big Springs Jct., W. Va.

Yard at Midland, W. Va.). Locals thus began or ended their runs in staging, not at South Fork, and some road crews both began and ended their runs in staging.

I grew uncomfortable with this approach and was "daylighting" the south end of North Yard so crews could "get on" (or off) their trains on a visible part of the railroad when the AM was abandoned (fig. 4-4).

When I designed the AM, I wasn't sure how much work a local crew would need to keep busy, but it turned out about right. A Local North crew would work a trailing-point pulpwood spur at Slate Falls, skip a facing-point

One AM crew member signed up for the Western Maryland "package" of jobs, which included running east and west locals and switching the Westvaco paper mill at North Durbin, W. Va. The session shown here was set in the late 1960s prior to the shift back to the steam-diesel transition era.

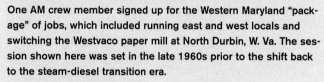

Passenger-train operations on the AM were low-key but still important. Trains 15 (shown here at Big Springs Jct., W. Va.) and 16 provided a connection between Chicago and Toledo via the Nickel Plate and Richmond and Norfolk via the Virginian & Ohio.

AM Staging

	← Inbound	Outbound →		Outbound →	← Inbound	
S12	Open	Open		Local South	No. 15	N1
S11	Hill Job	Open		CSXL-1	261	N2
S10		CXNL-1		No. 16	CXNE-1	N3
S9	CXSE-1	Open		Open	Open	N4
S8	CXSL-2	Mountain Dog		262	Mountain Dog	N5
S7	CSXL-1	CSNE-1		Open	Advance 95	N6
S6	No. 16	Advance 95		Open	AJN-1	N7
S5	Advance 94	261		CXSL-2	Open	N8
S4	262	Open		CXSE-1	AJN-3	N9
S3	Open	No. 15		Advance 94	CXNL-1	N10
S2	V&O Transfer	V&O transfer		SR-12	Open	N11
S1	V&O Transfer	V&O transfer		AJS-12	CV-1	N12
				No. 116	No. 115	N13

Mountain Grove

Kingswood Junction

North Yard

Hidden staging yards at both ends of the Allegheny Midland supported four hours of operation using a 6:1 clock ratio. Trains that left early and ran through to the other staging yard required an open track to receive them. Those that didn't move until late in the day blocked the use of that track by earlier inbound trains. Train assignments to all tracks were made in advance, but a few open tracks allowed for extras and other contingencies. Trains that originated in one staging yard, such as SR-12, but didn't terminate in the other ended their runs on the modeled part of the railroad (at Sunrise yard for SR-12). Trains such as AJN-1 and the Local North originated at Sunrise and terminated in staging.

spur at Gap Run, work a ramp track and brickyard at Lime Springs (and leave any Gap Run cars there for back-hauling by the Local South crew), work the WM interchange at North Durbin, set out cars for or pick up cars from the coal branch at Big Springs Jct., and make set outs for South Fork or the R&MC interchange at South Fork before tying up in North Yard (staging).

An important point to understand here is that the AM locals did not work the extensive paper mill tracks at North Durbin. The AM used trackage rights over the WM from Durbin Jct. (at the south edge of North Durbin) to Glady, so the WM's Mill Job crew worked the paper mill. Had there been too little work for the AM locals, I could have located the paper mill on the AM, but putting it on the WM created another job.

The railroad was dispatched by radio. The dispatcher sat at a Union Switch & Signal CTC machine (fig. 8-4), but it was never wired nor were signals installed by the time the AM was abandoned in 1999. (That machine is now at

the Howell Day Model Railroad Museum at NMRA headquarters in Chattanooga, Tenn.) The dispatcher could nonetheless use the board as a dispatching tool by moving the appropriate signal and switch levers to show how he planned to route each train. Train tags (markers) were hung on the levers to show clearance limits given to each train by radio.

The railroad developed over a quarter of a century and operated monthly for more than a decade. It met or exceeded my expectations, but it also made it very clear to me that a railroad should be designed with a specific type of operation in mind.

The AM was designed for

CTC operation, where the dispatcher could issue commands very quickly. I was therefore not overly concerned about distances between towns as long as I could separate them scenically. I would not have been satisfied with its design if timetable and train-order operation had been the goal, however, as trains could move between some towns much too rapidly. Crews could also readily see what was happening several towns down the line, making it a bit too tempting for them to move ahead without doing the homework required to determine what the timetable and any train orders actually allowed.

GAP RUN

CHAPTER TEN

What lies ahead

Fig. 10-1: We're just beginning to realize the potential of sound effects, not only on board our trains but in the surrounding tapestry. Tapes of telegraphed messages were played on the author's railroad, and crews on Andrew Dodge's On3 Denver, South Park & Pacific use a simple telegraphic code to move trains in a manual block system.

If I were truly clairvoyant, my time would be far too valuable for me to spend it writing hobby books, so take what follows with a large grain of salt. There are nevertheless some highly evident trends that will make operation more enjoyable, and they're worth a closer look.

Fig. 10-2: Unlike their prototypes, such as famed Nickel Plate Berkshire 779 taking water at Cleveland on June 15, 1957, model steam locomotives have endless supplies of "coal and water." Advances in DCC software will allow steam locomotives to measure coal and, more importantly, water usage. If the tender isn't refilled before the water is used up, the engine will stop. Lou Sabetto photo, collection of the author

Electronics

Not long ago, no one could imagine that three-quarters of a million transistors could be crammed onto a tiny chip, or that such a chip would be used to make model locomotives perform and sound more like their full-size counterparts on either a conventional DC- or a DCC-equipped railroad. But that has already happened, so imagine what lies just ahead.

Operation is affected in that technology is allowing us to focus more on the railroading and less on "model railroad thoughts." That is, we no longer have to look frantically along the fascia for the next toggle or rotary switch controlling our electrical block. Command control has eliminated such concerns. In fact, its use is warranted on small, one-or-two-locomotive railroads, as it offers sound, constant lighting, and full voltage to the rails at all times for better power pickup when starting or at slow speeds.

We can use sound effects

to operational advantage by, for example, whistling a warning to a train waiting for us on a passing track that we're carrying green flags, which means that at least one more section of our train is following on our schedule. Don't underestimate the value of sound; even a yard switcher sitting perfectly still seems to be doing something when you can hear its prime mover churning away inside or turbogenerator keeping the headlight burning. It seems to fill the void while you contemplate your next move, easing the pace of operations. Sound also adds "color" to the railroad—not just engine sounds but birds singing in the trees and the intermittent clicks of a telegraph emanating from a depot (fig. 10-1).

In the near future, Digital Command Control systems will know, for example, when your steam locomotive last took on more coal and water, and how much of each the tender can hold. It will constantly measure usage according to the work the

engine is doing and how long it has been doing it, and the engine will stop if you don't replenish the water or coal before the quantity has dropped to zero (fig. 10-2). This will force crews to make considered decisions about when to take coal and water vs. making a run for the next terminal in what could turn out to be a misguided quest to save time.

I also see the day when we will hold on-line operating sessions in our dens or home offices by way of high-capacity data links. Some creative soul will offer vacuum-formed half-size mock-ups of a variety of steam and diesel cab interiors, and we'll fit flat-panel video monitors into the window openings to ensure a good view ahead and to the rear. We'll contact a provider, mark up on-line for the era, railroad, and job of our choice, then assume the role of a dispatcher or road engineer. Tired? Mark off at the end of your run or trick, just like the pros do.

The hard part of this isn't the technology, which already

exists, albeit at a level that's still too expensive. Rather, the problem is that railroading is at times a very boring job, which is why crews occasionally drift off to sleep. How will we make the simulated versions of these jobs more fun? Important point: Virtual sessions will complement, not replace, operating sessions on scale model railroads. "Hard-copy" models have intrinsic value that no simulation can replace.

Right now, we're looking hard at the agent-operator's and even towerman's jobs. On the Maumee, the agent is charged with making business decisions about how many empties are needed and when loads are ready to pick up. What other interesting jobs have we been overlooking or under-utilizing?

Another area where electronics and the personal computer will increasingly shine is in the creation of databases. Companies such as ProTrak and organizations such as the NMRA's Operations SIG and some

railroad-specific historical societies have already created huge shipper databases. It will be increasingly easy to get railroad- and era-specific information about appropriate places to ship cars to and from. Some of these systems are already more than sophisticated enough to manage other operational aspects of our railroads, but marked improvements in user friendliness are still to come.

Much of the work will revolve around the vast capabilities of DCC. Whereas decoders were initially used primarily to control locomotives, special decoders can already control signaling and switch-motor applications. Want to enter a specific hidden staging track? Hit a number and activation button, and all related switches are aligned. No more complex rotary switches to wire and dial up. And some folks

are already talking about the day when we'll uncouple cars using onboard decoders.

There is a downside here in that wholesale automation is not a positive step toward better operation. Just because the engineer can throw a switch a scale hundred yards ahead of her train using a radio-controlled DCC throttle doesn't mean she should. Visualize how a professional railroader would do that work. A brakeman would either have to walk that distance to get that switch or, more likely, the engine would take the crew member down to it (fig. 10-3). The real pros excel at minimizing the number of steps used to do any given job, and part of the challenges and rewards of realistic operation is to emulate their actions. Even they can't wave magic wands to do work at a distance.

A few pioneers have used

laser scanning devices, like those in supermarkets, to detect the passage of cars. This allows computer databases to know how and when cars are being moved, rather than assuming humans put them exactly where and when the computer-generated switch list said they should. This, in turn, allows subsequent switch lists to accurately reflect car locations. I therefore expect scanners aimed at model railroad operating needs to be marketed.

Improvements in signaling systems are also needed. We need true plug-and-play systems before signaling, from ABS to CTC, is used extensively by the average modeler. Considering the major visual and realism enhancements that signals offer to the typical layout, this will be a major step forward. Train-detection devices that help us keep track of trains

Fig. 10-3: To operate realistically, one has to consider the actions of miniature humans going about their jobs. Railroaders can't walk from one end of a yard to the other in a few seconds to get a switch or locate a car. If they need to go somewhere, they'll hop on the engine and let the engineer take them there, or they'll have the yard engine pull an entire track filled with cars past the place they're standing to see what's in it. Modeling jobs well is increasingly the focus of the most progressive operating layouts.

operating on hidden trackage such as helixes, staging yards, and so on also need to be offered as part of these plug-and-play systems.

"Finer-scale" modeling
The ongoing trend toward ever finer scale models is

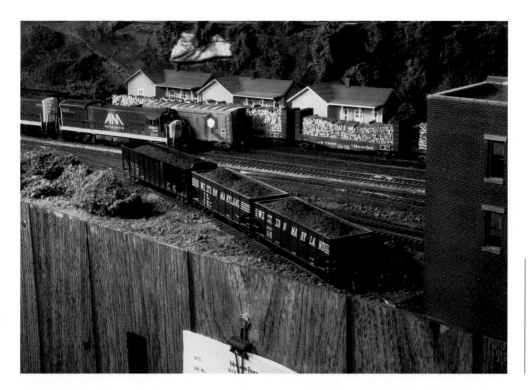

Fig. 10-4: Although this truncated system is assumed to extend off the edge of the layout into an unmodeled "aisle-side" industry, there's really no telling where realistic operation can take you on your model railroad.

apparent, but as I've already documented, this carries the potential of greater damage to equipment during operating sessions. Manufacturers are addressing this with more rugged plastics for handrails, grab irons, and steps that are also closer to scale thicknesses. But modelers who cut off the "air hoses" on magnetic couplers to enhance their appearance are then faced with the need to uncouple cars with a skewer or other insertion tool, and car-end details may be damaged. A better system is still needed and, thanks to DCC, may be just down the track.

A relatively recent development in HO scale is the production of close-to-scale magnetic couplers. This makes sense, as narrow-gaugers and N scale modelers have been using small knuckle couplers; if they work for them, they should work with HO standard-gauge equipment. There are concerns to address, but such developments are commendable and exciting to watch.

There is a similar effort afoot to use closer-to-scale wheels in HO. The NMRA's RP-25 wheel profiles (there are several) provide guidance here, but the main issue on the table is whether we should stick with a known wheel width that has served us well for decades or follow the trend toward greater realism. I found that narrower (code 88) wheels from NorthWest Short Line worked well on the Allegheny Midland, even though the railroad—especially the hand-laid turnouts—were built with the "standard" code 110 wheels in mind. And now one leading manufacturer is offering code 88 wheels on ready-to-use HO freight cars.

My guess is that more manufacturers will therefore follow the lead of NWSL and Atlas by reducing wheel widths, at least on their premium-level equipment, just as Kadee has done with scale couplers on their highly detailed, ready-to-run HO freight cars. But a railroad that operates poorly is going to gather a lot of dust, so we have to edge away from today's norms only as we weigh perceived improve-

ments against possible complications.

Let there be light

There's no need for day-night effects for realistic operation, but many operators are intrigued by the possibilities of night sessions, not to mention the visual drama as day eases into night and vice versa. But builders of large layouts can't afford to introduce vast numbers of incandescent lights into the railroad room because of the heat they generate, and fluorescents remain difficult to dim completely and inexpensively.

That said, I believe a solution is near at hand as fluorescent lighting developments continue at a rapid pace. This is, after all, an ecological concern, as incandescent bulbs waste energy and emit reddish light in other rooms of the house as well. Someone will offer a complete dimming system tied to a series of analog or digital clocks (depending on the era you model) that will keep everything in sync. Since DCC throttles already have

fast-time clock LCD read-outs, this isn't a major hurdle.

In short, the big news of tomorrow will simply be the integration of everything from car and train movements to paperwork to lighting effects to signaling and communication systems. Thanks to the NMRA's pioneering efforts to develop DCC standards, we have a solid platform upon which to build. I, for one, am excited about what the future has in store for realistic operation.

Appendix

Absolute-Permissive Block: APB circuits can determine the direction of a train between passing tracks and set all opposing signals to red. APB also allows signals behind the train to clear as it passes from block to block.

Absolute signal: A number plate on the signal mast identifies a permissive signal. The lack of a number plate means the signal is absolute: "Stop and stay stopped."

Aisle-side industry: A partially modeled (or not modeled at all) industry or interchange served by a siding truncated at the front edge of the benchwork. The same trick can be used on the backdrop side of the main by having the siding or interchange track disappear behind terrain, foliage, structures, or backdrop.

Aspect: The appearance of a signal conveying its indication; the color of the light or the position of the blade or a row of lights on a signal.

Assigned-service cars: Cars in assigned service travel a regular route loaded and empty and are often equipped with special loading devices such as racks to hold auto parts.

Automatic Block System: A series of consecutive blocks governed by block signals actuated by a train, engine, or certain conditions affecting the use of a block.

Big hole: An emergency brake application made by moving the air-brake handle so as to open the large trainline vent port, or "big hole." "Dump the air" means the same thing.

Bill of lading: A legal contract of carriage prepared by a shipper and given to the railroad; the railroad uses it to prepare a waybill.

Blocking cars: Grouping cuts of cars while switching by like destinations, then arranging the blocks for efficient switching at subsequent yards. Entire trains may comprise a single block, as a train of perishables heading for a single destination.

Bridge traffic: Also called "overhead" traffic, meaning through cars that traverse an entire railroad en route to a more distant destination. Railroads win bridge traffic by showing they can consistently move it rapidly between connecting railroads.

Car card: A 2″ x 4″ or 3″ x 5″ card with a pocket for waybills used in the "card order" car-forwarding system.

Classification lights: Carried on locomotives (and sometimes mistakenly called "markers," which denote the end of a train) to denote class: extinguished for regular trains, green for another section following, and white for extra. Flags may be used in the daytime.

Clean-out track: A yard track where cars are cleaned before being reloaded. It serves as an "industry" in that cars have to be moved to and/or from the clean-out track during an operating session.

Clearance card: No train can occupy a main track without the dispatcher's okay, which is issued as a clearance (often called Clearance Form A, fig. A-1). If orders or messages are issued with the clearance, the quantity and specific numbers of the orders and quantity of messages will be specified. There may also be a notation about the status of the next block.

Command control: Analog or, increasingly, digital control signals sent through the rails to decoders in each locomotive, and only the locomotive for which a signal is coded will respond. The commands from each hand-held throttle may be sent over a wire tether or via infrared or radio signals to a central command station, then via bus wires and feeders to the rails. Rail-Lynx IR signals go directly to decoders on the locomotives.

Conductor: Traditionally, the boss of the train, even though the engineer runs it.

Cornfield meet: A head-on collision between two trains, which occasionally occurs out in the country alongside a cornfield.

Dark territory: An unsignaled section of a main line.

Demurrage: An increasing-with-time rental fee that generally kicks in 24 hours after a car has been spotted for loading or 48 hours for unloading, an incentive to get the car moving again. Weekends and holidays are not counted.

Double the hill: Trains that have extra tonnage or encounter poor rail conditions (wet leaves, deep snow) may stall on a hill and be unable to restart. If a helper engine is not at hand, the crew may split the train into two or more sections and double or triple the hill.

Drill: To switch cars; also used as a term meaning local or way freight.

Drop: Rather than running around a car, a crew can leave the car behind the engine, accelerate the engine and car slightly, uncouple the car, then accelerate the engine rapidly to get ahead of the car. After the engine passes over the facing-point switch, the switch is thrown to route the car into the siding. Timing is obviously critical to avoid problems. A drop is extremely difficult to do with models.

Extra train: A freight or passenger train not listed in the employee timetable is run as an extra. An extra train is usually created with a "Form G" train order: "Eng 123 run extra A to B". A passenger extra is similarly created: "Eng 234 run Passenger Extra A to D". A work extra is created with an order allowing it to work between two specified points for a period of time: "Eng 456 work extra A to D 645 AM until 545 PM". Its orders can state that it has right over all trains, as in the case of a wreck train hurrying to the site of a derailment. Right of track orders are usually not combined with Form G orders.

Facing-point switch: If the locomotive approaching a switch encounters the points before it rolls over the frog, that's calling a facing-point switch. Note that a trailing-point switch for a westbound train becomes a facing-point switch for an eastbound train.

FRED: Flashing rear-end device used in lieu of a manned caboose. First used in the '70s.

Grade signal: As an aid to heavy upgrade trains, which can be stopped quickly, stop-and-proceed signals may have a "G" (for grade) plate affixed to allow ascending trains to pass signals indicating "stop" at a restricted speed.

Grand pull, grand shove: It would be unsafe to switch cars in a large industrial complex, so crews typically enter the plant and make a "grand pull" of all outbound cars plus any cars blocking their exit. These cars are taken to a nearby yard where the outbound cars are switched out. The inbound cars and cars that were in the way are then arranged in spot order for efficient switching, and a "grand shove" is made into the plant.

Ground throw: See *Switchstand*.

Hand throw: See *Switchstand*.

Highball: Signals were formerly balls on masts, and a ball at the top indicated "proceed." The term is still used to indicate that it's okay to go ahead.

Hog law: Just as railroads cannot keep livestock in stock cars more than 28 consecutive hours (36 under some circumstances), today train crews cannot be kept on duty more than 12 hours. The original hours-of-service law, jokingly referred to as the "hog law," allowed for 16 hours of continuous duty, which was later reduced to 14 hours and then to 12. When a crew's time expires, they "go dead on the law" and cannot move the train another inch. Every effort is made to get the train off the main line before that time, but when severe congestion or bad weather occurs, that isn't always possible.

Indication: What a signal tells a train crewman to do, such as "proceed."

Interlocking: An arrangement of signals and signal appliances interconnected so that their movements must succeed each other in proper sequence and for which interlocking rules are in effect. It may be operated manually or automatically.

Intermodal: Truck plus train (and perhaps air and/or ship as well), such as TOFC (trailer on flat car) or COFC (container on flat car).

LCL: Less than Carload Lot freight, like freight-forwarding companies today. LCL cars, often boxcars or rider cars located behind the engine or just ahead of the caboose, were filled at major freight houses. Parcels ranging from small boxes to major appliances were wrestled out of the cars at stations along the line as the local paused by the depot. Entire cars or even trains filled with LCL were moved between major terminals.

Local freight: A freight train, scheduled or extra, that stops at stations along a division to perform switching work, thus allowing through freights to maintain faster schedules.

Loose car: Railroads would prefer to move traffic in entire trains, called unit trains. But much general merchandise traffic comprises one or a small number of "loose" cars from a shipper to a consignee (receiver). Retrieving these loose cars, typically by a local freight, and switching them into trains in yards is time-consuming, hence very expensive—but fun for modelers!

Manual block: A system of block signals operated by operators who control the use of blocks between operator stations but do not supersede the superiority of trains unless otherwise provided.

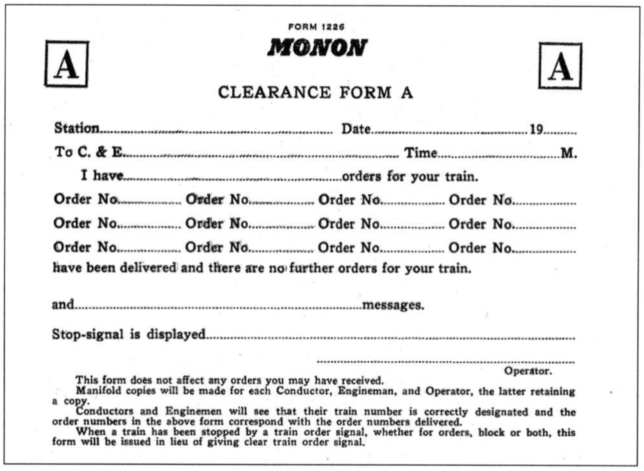

Fig. A-1: Monon clearance card (Clearance Form A)

Markers: Lights or flags denoting the end of the train. May be carried on the back of a tender, the front of a locomotive when running in reverse, on a caboose or the last passenger car, or mounted on the last coupler.

Midnight shove: To avoid being assessed per diem charges, railroads worked hard to get cars across their system and onto the rails of connecting roads at interchanges or yards. These charges were assessed at midnight, so a lot of delivery activity took place as that hour approached.

MT or MTY: An "empty" car.

Name: The word used in talking about a signal, as "clear."

OS: Means "on sheet" or "out of station," as is an operator saying to the dispatcher, "OS Lafayette." (Pauses for dispatcher's acknowledgment.) "Train 62 by at 5:15 p.m." The call is made after the caboose, not the engine, passes the station.

Patrol: See *Local freight*.

Peddler freight: See *Local freight*.

Per diem: "Per day" rental charges assessed to the railroad a foreign-road car is on at midnight each day. "Incentive" per diem was created in the 1970s to allow newly built boxcars to earn a higher rate of return if certain conditions were met, thereby increasing the number of cars available for loading.

Permissive signal: Designated with a number plate, its stop indication means stop, then proceed at restricted speed. Designated with a "P" plate, it can either mean the same thing, or it can mean proceed at restricted speed without stopping.

Poling pole and pocket: Cars could be moved on an adjacent track by inserting a long, heavy pole in pockets on the corner of the locomotive's pilot and the end sill of a freight car. This was a dangerous practice, as the pole could slip or break, but it survived well into the diesel era. Theoretically, it could be done on a model railroad using a tapered toothpick as a pole.

Pool power: Rather than taking time to change diesel locomotive consists at end-to-end junctions between railroads, power was allowed to continue on with the train. The owner of a pooled unit was paid for its usage by horsepower hours or by other means.

Private-owner cars: Cars with reporting marks ending with an X, as GARX for General American Car's reefer fleet, that are paid for by the railroads to the owners on the basis of mileage rather than by per diem charges.

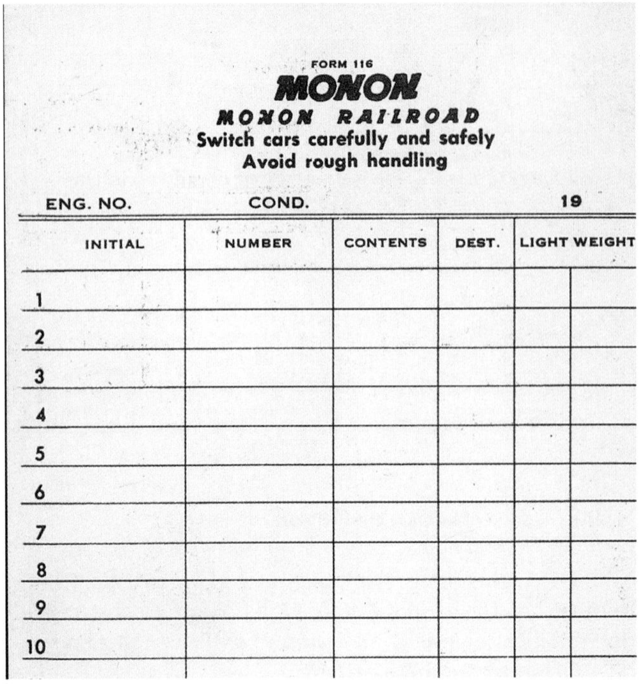
FORM 116

MONON

MONON RAILROAD

Switch cars carefully and safely

Avoid rough handling

ENG. NO. COND. 19

	INITIAL	NUMBER	CONTENTS	DEST.	LIGHT WEIGHT
1					
2					
3					
4					
5					
6					
7					
8					
9					
10					

Fig. A-2: Monon switch list

Proper: Freight cars billed for an in-town destination (as at a division point), or cars in a freight billed for delivery *at* the next division point, rather than beyond it.
RIP track: "Repair-in-place" track, where minor repairs were quickly made.
Scheduled train: A train listed in the employee timetable. Scheduled trains are usually ranked by class from first to third or even fourth. See *Superiority.*
Shorts: Cars destined for the adjoining division, usually to be delivered by a local.
Station: Not a depot (structure) but a place where time is shown in a timetable.
Superiority: *The Standard Code of Operating Rules* explains superiority of trains using several rules:

Rule S-71 [S for single track]: A train is superior to another by right, class, or direction. Right is conferred by train order; class and direction are specified in the timetable. Right is superior to class or direction. Direction is superior between trains of the same class. [East- and northbound trains are usually denoted as being superior to west- and southbound trains.]

Rule 72: First-class trains are superior to second-class trains, second to third, and so on.

Rule S-73: Trains in the direction specified by timetable are superior to trains of the same class in the opposite direction.

Rule 73: Extra trains are inferior to regular trains (that is, trains authorized by timetable schedules).

The dispatcher can change the superiority of trains by train orders, such as "Form S-C," right-of-track order, such as "No 9 has right over No 10 Frankfort to Cayuga" or a "Form E" time order, such as "No 10 wait at Cayuga for No 9 until 301 AM". This helps no. 9 advance against a late-running no. 10.
Switch and turnout: A *turnout* lets a train diverge from one route to another. The movable part of a turnout is called a *switch.* This includes the switch points and a switch rod to connect them to the locally or remotely controlled device that allows them to be moved. You can therefore "line a switch," but you can't "throw a turnout" (it weighs too much and is spiked down!). You'll hear railroaders say "get the switch" or "take the switch to the engine lead," which is consistent with the idea that the switch is the part of the turnout that moves to allow such route changes.
Switch list: A common type of list is prepared on a thin card-stock form, typically 4¼″ x 11″ in size, where cuts of cars are listed in their existing sequence showing their reporting marks, number, contents, and destination. The yardmaster then marks which track each car should be switched into to block them in the desired order (fig. A-2). "Push-pull" is another form of switch list.
Switch motor: A switch motor allows the points to be controlled electrically or pneumatically by a towerman or by a dispatcher using a CTC machine at a remote location. Also refers to motors that move switch points on model railroads; Tortoise is one popular brand.
Switch stand: A switch stand lets a trainman move the points, and it stands tall so trains coming down the main track can see which way the switch is lined at some distance (fig. A-3). Lower-level mechanisms for other than main tracks are called hand or ground throws.
Throughs: Cars destined for the next division point or beyond.
Timetable: A timetable establishes schedules for trains and contains special instructions that may amend the Book of Rules. Trains not listed in the timetable are operated as extras.
Trackage rights: One train may run its trains over another's tracks by paying a prearranged "toll" or wheelage charge, as it is based upon the number of cars being moved. The home road usually reserves the right to switch on-line customers.
Train: A locomotive or more than one locomotive coupled, with or without cars, displaying markers.
Train sheet: The large sheets of paper used by dispatchers to keep track of trains, including the locomotive number(s), crews, time on duty, and number of loads and empties. Times are recorded in each train's column as it is OSed by operators along the line. CTC machines generate such sheets mechanically.
Trick: An 8-hour work shift; there are three tricks per day, generally beginning at midnight, 8 a.m., and 4 p.m.
Turn: A train that leaves a terminal, travels to a point short of the next terminal, and returns to the original terminal.
Turn-around local: Local freight that begins and ends its daily run in the same terminal.
Unit train: A train of the same type of car headed toward one destination, such as hoppers loaded with coal headed for a power plant. Other unit trains may handle crude oil, grain, fertilizer, or even orange juice.
Varnish: Nickname for passenger train derived from the days when wood-sided passenger cars were painted, then varnished to achieve a high luster.
Wash out: Hand signal for *Stop!* It describes the side-to-side swinging arc of a trainman's arm or lantern.
Waybill: A document prepared by a railroad based on information conveyed by the shipper in a bill of lading. It provides all required information for the movement of a load in a freight car: car type, number and reporting marks, points of

Fig. A-3: The green diagonal clearly shows the switch is lined for the main.

origin and destination, routing, lading with weight. and whether the shipment is perishable. Waybills travel in the possession of the conductor.

Way freight: see *Local freight*.

Wheel report: List prepared by the conductor from waybill information showing all cars moved in a train.

Section A-2: Book of Rules

Books of Rules are often sold at swap meets. Acquiring one for your favorite railroad(s) is worthwhile. Here are some of the rules commonly used to operate a model railroad:

Rule G: Intoxicants not permitted on railroad property or in crew members.

Rule 71: See "Superiority" in Appendix section A-1: Terminology

Rule 72: See "Superiority" in Appendix section A-1: Terminology

Rule 73: See "Superiority" in Appendix section A-1: Terminology

Rule 82: Timetable schedules are in effect for 12 hours after their time at each station unless fulfilled, annulled by train order, or abolished by general order for the life of the timetable. Regular trains more than 12 hours behind either their scheduled arriving or leaving time at any station lose both right and schedule, and can thereafter proceed only as authorized by train order.

Rule 82: A train may not leave its initial station on any subdivision, or a junction, or pass from two or more tracks to single track, or leave CTC territory until it has been ascertained that all superior trains have arrived or left.

Rule 87: An inferior train must clear the time of opposing superior trains by not less than five minutes. An inferior train failing to clear the main track by the time required must be given flag protection as prescribed by Rule 99.

Rule 92: A train must not leave a station in advance of its scheduled departure time.

Rule 99: When a train stops under circumstances in which it may be overtaken by another train, or when other conditions require flag protection, a member of the crew must go out immediately a sufficient distance to ensure full protection. The front of the train must be protected in the same way when necessary.

Rule 251: [ABS rule] On portions of the railroad and on designated tracks specified by timetable, trains moving with the current of traffic will run with reference to other trains in the same direction by block signals whose indications supersede the superiority of trains.

Rule 261: [CTC rule] On portions of the railroad and on designated tracks specified by timetable, trains will be governed by block signals whose indications supersede the superiority of trains for both opposing and following movements on the same track.

Section A-3: Standard forms for train orders

Train orders are worded according to strict constraints based on hard-won experience. Punctuation and even hours (1200) are not used. Here are some typical forms:

Form A (meet order): "No 9 meet No 10 at Cayuga" [engine numbers may also be specified]

Form B (trains passing): "No 1 Eng 177 pass No 43 Eng 659 at Cayuga"

Form C (giving right): "No 9 has right over No 10"

Form D (giving right in same direction): "No 98 has right over No 10 Frankfort to Cayuga"

Form E (time order): "No 10 run 30 mins late Cayuga to Ridge Farm". May also tell a train to wait at a certain station for another train, or give a schedule of times at a series of stations.

Form G (extra trains): "Eng 185 run extra Frankfort to Charleston" or "Eng 185 run extra Frankfort to Cayuga and return to Frankfort"

Form J (holding order): "Hold No 10" or "Hold all eastward trains"

Form K (annulling schedule or section): "No 9 is annulled Cayuga to Charleston"

Form L (annulling order): "Order no 12 is annulled"

Form P (superseding orders): "No 9 meet No 10 at Humrick instead of Cayuga"

Section A-4: Operating information resources

E-mail addresses frequently change, and suppliers enter or drop out of the market. Contact *Model Railroader* Magazine for an update if you have trouble finding the necessary paperwork or software. These listings were correct as of the publication date:

Organizations, suppliers:

- Layout Design Special Interest Group of the NMRA: Douglas B. Gurin, 605 Tennessee Ave., Alexandria VA 22305. Website: www.ldsig.org. The LD-SIG publishes an informative *Layout Design Journal*. Dues are $15.
- Old Line Graphics: 1604 Woodwell, Silver Spring MD 20906 <oldlinegraphics@erols.com>. OLG supplies the four-cycle waybills, car cards, and associated forms.
- Operations SIG of the NMRA: P.O. Box 872, Arlington Heights IL 60006. Website: www.opsig.com. The OP-SIG's informative magazine is called *The Dispatcher's Office*. Dues are $15 U.S. and Canada, $23 overseas. Also sells car cards and waybills.
- Photo Electric: P.O. Box 13657, Salem OR 97309. Phone 503-370-9828. E-mail: espee@qwest.net. Photo Electric produces US&S CTC machine parts and custom cabinets.
- ProTrak: 50 Mill St., Baden, Ontario, Canada N0B 1G0.

Phone (evenings, weekends): 519-634-5436. Website: www.protrak.cc. E-mail: jim@protrak.cc. ProTrak offers a software package and comprehensive database covering all aspects of operation.

- Rail Graphics: 1183 N. Lancaster Circle, South Elgin IL 60177. Rail Graphics has rule books tailored for modelers.
- Railway Signaling Technical and Historical Society, signaling SIG of the NMRA: Ron Ferrel, 1126 Cedar Hollow Dr., Pocatello, ID 83204 <Railway-Signaling@yahoogroups.com>. The group's newsletter is called *Clear Block*.
- Quaker Valley Software: P.O. Box 814, Shillington PA 19607-0814. Website: www.quaker-valley.com. QVS software allows the user to produce customized waybills, car cards, and other useful forms.

Books and magazine articles:

- Abbey, Wallace: "It's Your Railroad" in *I Like Trains* (Kalmbach; out of print)
- Armstrong, John: *The Railroad—What It Is, What It Does* (Simmons-Boardman, Omaha, Neb.)
- Armstrong, John: *Track Planning for Realistic Operation, Third Edition* (Kalmbach)
- Brunner, Edward J.: "Of Rule 93, Form S-C, and the Bow and Arrow Country," July 1980 *Trains*
- Bryan, Frank: "Farewell to the Train Order," November 1986 *Trains*
- Chubb, Bruce: *How to Operate Your Model Railroad* (Kalmbach; out of print)
- Chubb, Bruce: "Centralized Traffic Control for the Sunset Valley," January 1984 *Model Railroader*
- Chubb, Bruce: "Signals on the Sunset Valley," October 1970 *Model Railroader*
- Darnaby, Bill: "Card-order operation for passenger trains," October 1993 *Model Railroader*
- Darnaby, Bill: "Designing a timetable for the Maumee Route," January 1993 *Model Railroader*
- Droege, John A.: *Freight Trains and Terminals*, reprinted by the National Model Railroad Association, 4121 Cromwell Road, Chattanooga TN 37421
- Frailey, Fred: "South End Desk," September 1986 *Trains*
- Hediger, Jim: "Wheel reports for easy operation," May 1984 *Model Railroader*
- Holbrook, Dan: "Locomotive and caboose cards," February 1992 *Model Railroader*
- Josserand, Peter: *The Rights of Trains* (Simmons-Boardman, 1809 Capitol Ave., Omaha NE 68102)
- King, Steve: series on timetable and train-order operation in Operation SIG's *The Dispatcher's Office*
- Morgan, David P.: "Tide 470," April 1956 *Trains*
- Petersen, Gary: "Simplified CTC Signals," July 1988 *Model Railroader*

- Ravenscroft, Ed: "Operation with CCT," July 1964 *Model Railroader*
- Ravenscroft, Ed: "Waytacks on the new GSV," February 1979 *Railroad Model Craftsman*
- Schuchmann, Walt: "String-line train scheduling," June 1995 *Model Railroader*
- Tajibnapis, Will: "Timetable and train order operation," August 1999 *Model Railroader*
- Thompson, Ken: "Centralized Traffic Control for the Cat Mountain & Santa Fe," May 1984 *Model Railroader*

Section A-5: Common freight-car types

The Association of American Railroads has assigned short-hand terms for each type of freight car, and many modelers use these to save space on waybills and car cards. Most are obvious, but "L" is derived from "speciaL," a covered hopper being a special type of hopper. Here are some common designations:

FC: flat car that carries trucks and trailers
FD: depressed-center flat car
FM: ordinary flat car
GB: ordinary gondola (GA has a drop bottom)
HM: ordinary open two-bay hopper
HT: ordinary open triple or quad hopper
LO: covered hopper
LP: pulpwood car
RA: brine-tank refrigerator car
RBL: insulated reefer without icc bunkers or ventilating system
RP: mechanical reefer
SM: single-deck stock car (SC is convertible to single or double deck)
TA: ordinary tank car, if there is such a thing
XAP: auto-parts boxcar
XM: ordinary general-service boxcar

Section A-6: Common passenger-car types

Passenger equipment can usually be identified by noting its window arrangement. A diner, for example, typically has some smaller windows along one end where the cramped kitchen is located. Here are some common designations:

BE: Heavyweight baggage car
PB.: Heavyweight coach
PB: Lightweight coach
CA: Heavyweight combination passenger-baggage car
MA: Heavyweight railway post office car
PA: Lightweight dining car
PB (dome): Lightweight dome coach
PO: Heavyweight observation car
PS: Heavyweight sleeping car (Pullman)
PS: Lightweight sleeping car (Pullman)